Diseases and Pests of

Ⲛ   ⌐

Date Due

With _____ _____ _____ ᴇcts,
Ⴝ _____ _____ _____ ┤

BRODART, CO.   Cat. No. 23-233   Printed in U.S.A.

British Library Cataloguing-in-Publication Data
A catalogue record for this book is available from the
British Library

Mushrooms

A mushroom (or toadstool) is the fleshy, spore-bearing fruiting body of a fungus, typically produced above ground on soil or on its food source. The standard for the name 'mushroom' is the cultivated white button mushroom, *Agaricus bisporus*; hence the word 'mushroom' is most often applied to those fungi (Basidiomycota, Agaricomycetes) that have a stem (stipe), a cap (pileus), and gills (lamellae, sing. lamella) or pores on the underside of the cap.

The terms 'mushroom' and 'toadstool' go back centuries and were never precisely defined, nor was there consensus on application. The term 'toadstool' was often, but not exclusively, applied to poisonous mushrooms or to those that have the classic umbrella-like cap-and-stem form. Between 1400 and 1600 AD, the terms *tadstoles, frogstooles, frogge stoles, tadstooles, tode stoles, toodys hatte, paddockstool, puddockstool, paddocstol, toadstoole, and paddockstooles* sometimes were used synonymously with *mushrum, muscheron, mousheroms, mussheron, or musserouns.* The term 'mushroom' and its variations may have been derived from the French word *mousseron* in reference to moss (*mousse*).

Identifying mushrooms requires a basic understanding of their macroscopic structure. Most are Basidiomycetes and gilled. Their spores, called basidiospores, are produced on the gills and fall in a fine rain of powder from under the caps as a result. As a result, for most mushrooms, if the cap is cut off and placed gill-side-down overnight, a powdery impression reflecting the shape of the gills (or pores, or spines, etc.) is formed (when the fruit body is sporulating). The colour of the powdery print, called a spore print, is used to help classify mushrooms and can help to identify them. Spore print colours include white (most common), brown, black, purple-brown, pink, yellow, and creamy, but almost never blue, green, or red.

While modern identification of mushrooms is quickly becoming molecular, the standard methods for identification are still used by most and have developed into a fine art, harking back to medieval times and the Victorian era. The presence of juices upon breaking, bruising reactions, odours, tastes, shades of colour, habitat, habit, and season are all considered by both amateur and professional mycologists. Tasting and smelling mushrooms carries its own hazards though, because of poisons and allergens. In general, identification to genus can often be accomplished in the field using a local mushroom guide. Identification to species, however, requires more effort; and one must remember that a mushroom develops from a button stage into a mature structure, and only the latter can provide certain characteristics needed for the identification of the species.

However, over-mature specimens lose features and cease producing spores. Many novices have mistaken humid water marks on paper for white spore prints, or discoloured paper from oozing liquids on lamella edges for coloured spore prints. A number of species of mushrooms are poisonous; although some resemble certain edible species, consuming them could be fatal. Eating mushrooms gathered in the wild is risky and should not be undertaken by individuals not knowledgeable in mushroom identification, unless the individuals limit themselves to a relatively small number of good edible species, that are visually distinctive. People who collect mushrooms for consumption are known as 'mycophagists', and the act of collecting them for such is known as mushroom hunting, or simply 'mushrooming'. Have fun!

Contents

DISEASES

MYCOGONE *perniciosa* Magn., the "Bubble" Disease*, is a mold-like parasite attacking the mushrooms at any stage, but not the spawn. Mushrooms attacked in the early stages become round balls or "bubbles", rotting in the center. Older mushrooms will become deformed. The fungus attacks the gills at once, and almost the first sign is the deformed crooked gills. The source of the fungus is the diseased mushrooms and infected spent compost from previous crops. It is controlled by careful cleaning, and fumigation of the house with sulphur or formaldehyde before filling; and the selection of soil for casing at some distance from the plant(200 yds.) and where no spent compost has been put.

Sulphur fumigation is to be preferred to formaldehyde on account of its lower cost and the certainty of elimination of insects. Refined stick or "roll" sulphur should be used, as it burns more easily than the crude grade. Where small quantities are to be burned, "flowers of sulphur" is a very handy grade. It is carried out as follows. The house is tightly closed (except one door) and strips of paper are pasted over all cracks. Sulphur in the amount of five pounds for each 1000 cubic feet of space in the building is weighed out, and burned in pans in the aisles of the house. The pans should be five inches in depth and each pan may contain enough sulphur to fill it about one and one half inches deep. All woodwork within three feet of a pan, or above or below it, should be protected with sheets of iron.

If formaldehyde is preferred on account of the lesser fire risk, the house should be closed in the same way, and the formaldehyde vaporized in a metal barrel or water boiler over a fire. The gases are led into the house through a pipe. The usual treatment is with two quarts of 40 per cent formaldehyde (formalin) for each 1000 cubic feet of space. The container should be boiled dry.

* CHARLES, VERA K., & POPENOE, C. H., Circular 27, U. S. Dept. Agri., Feb. 1928.

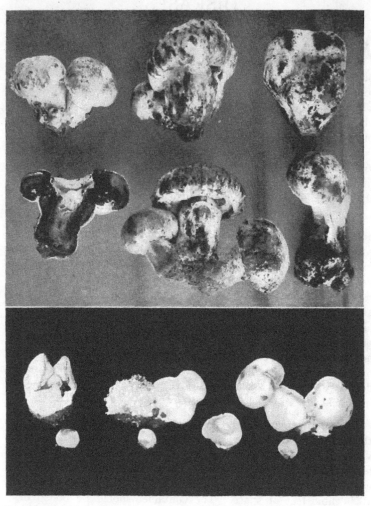

The Bubble disease turns mushrooms or clumps of mushrooms into shapeless lumps. The "bubbles" often split while growing. Exudation of drops of liquid is characteristic, as seen in two of the lower specimens. Diseased and healthy mushrooms may grow in the same clump. Tiny "bubbles" as shown in the bottom row are produced toward the end of the crop, usually associated with insect injury to the "pinheads." Upper photograph loaned by the U. S. Department of Agriculture.

This fumigation is not specific against insects, but will usually eliminate them before the end of twenty four hours if the house is tight.

The gases should be left in the closed building two days or longer, and before the building is opened the surrounding ground should be treated. Formaldehyde sprays are used for this purpose, but they evaporate very quickly, and the writer prefers a liberal soaking with mercuric chloride. Four pounds of this material is dissolved in 50 gallons of water, and sprayed on the ground and up the side of the mushroom house around the doors. An ordinary sprinkling can is used, for the chemical is hard on metals and will eat through a spray outfit in a short time. Mercuric chloride is a powerful poison.

After fumigation is carried out, the chief danger of infection is in the soil. The spores can live four years in the soil, and are easily carried by water. They are not known to be spread by winds, on account of their weight. Care must be taken to keep them from the water supply. They may be killed in infected soil by raising the temperature to 140°F. for two hours as described in Chapter VIII. Diseased mushrooms must be picked off and destroyed as soon as they appear. Any house seriously infected should be carried at 50°F., at which temperature the fungus is less active. The varieties of mushrooms differ in susceptibility, the Pure White being least susceptible. Careful growers have no fear of the Mycogone.

Deformed mushrooms, with a growth resembling gills in various places over the cap, are sometimes produced on the first "break" of mushrooms. All bad cases which have been studied seem to be the result of accidental contact of the casing soil with mineral oil or kerosene, or the spraying of houses with kerosene insect killers. The latter must not be used. This type of growth is also found in the first break of crops which have been held back by dryness of soil. These mushrooms are edible and there is no reason why they should not be used. They seldom appear after the first break.

The "Truffle" disease, which has been described in Chapter IX as a weed mold, may be a true disease of the mycelium. It is not known to develop except in beds well run with spawn, and certainly kills the spawn wherever it grows. It is therefore correct to call this organism a disease.

Spotted mushrooms infected with *Bacterium tolaasi* (Paine) Elliott, and Fungus spot.

Bacterial Spot, *Bacterium tolaasi* (Paine) Elliott, is a disease present in practically all plants. The surface layers of tissue of the mushroom cap break down and turn darker, eventually becoming black. The infection is usually in irregular spots where it is inoculated into the mushroom by insects. The spots become slightly sunken. The virulence of the bacterium is not great, and spots often heal as the mushroom grows. The conditions which favor infection and growth of the spots are high temperatures, high humidity, and insect prevalence. The disease is always commonest at the end of the crop. It is kept to a minimum by low temperature and low humidity, and prompt drying of young mushrooms after watering.

There are at least two other Spot diseases, one a fungus and the other a bacterium which is found in very small but deep hollows in the caps. The fungus spot resembles the *Bacterium tolaasi* spot, but the third does not darken, the bacteria in the depression being a glistening white. The spots are often completely covered by the "skin" or surface tissues of the mushroom.

These organisms are all probably carried by certain insects. The channels made in mushroom stems by the fly larvae often blacken with the growth of the *Bacterium tolaasi*. The white bacterial spot is often found in the hollows made by mites, and both are suspected to follow the attacks of nematodes or eelworms.

In caves and cellars the spot organisms may become serious even when insects are not common. More liberal ventilation and more careful watering will usually serve to reduce the damage.

"WEED MOLDS"

THESE organisms attack the compost and prevent spawn or mushroom growth. For want of accurate information common names will be used. The best known of these is the "Plaster Mold", the white mycelium of which, growing in the bed, has an intensely pungent odor. When the mold fruits, a dense white patch appears on the surface and in the manure, and this turns brown from the center outward with the production of "sclerotia", resting bodies so large that they feel like fine sand. Although carried to some extent by insects, and inoculated into the beds by them if the beds are uncased and damp on the surface (which they should not be), the source is usually the cooler parts of the compost heap. The mold appears to be more common in wet weather. Its control is simple; the mold is killed by temperatures above 125°F., and a filled house which goes above that point in all parts is free of it. If it appears in beds which are not too wet, the spawn can overcome it, and will even produce mushrooms through the brown patches of sclerotia. When this mold appears, the grower should spread bone-dry soil on the patches, and when the mold grows through it, remove the soil and repeat the treatment. It will mature and die out in dry conditions, and the spawn can then grow through it. Where the mold appears on the casing soil the soil may be removed and replaced until the mold ceases to grow.

The "Flour mold" or "White Plaster mold", *Monilia fimicola* Cost. & Matr., is not known to be present in the compost heap, and seldom appears on the beds until two or three weeks after spawning.* Without much odor, the white mycelium usually grows close to the surface in wet compost and produces flour-like patches of white or pinkish spores in the upper layers and on the surface. The compost attacked fails to run full with spawn and will not

* CHARLES, VERA K., & POPENOE, C. H., Circular 27, U. S. Dept. Agric., Feb. 1928 (Section headed Plaster Mold).

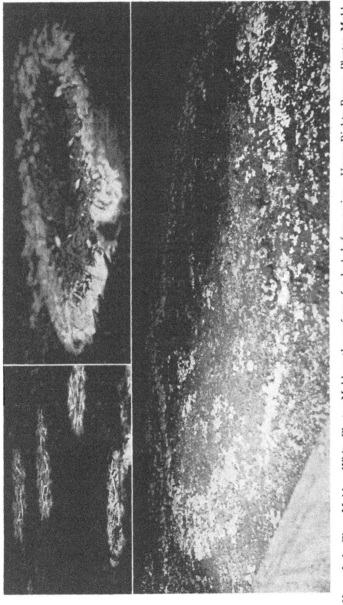

Upper Left: Flour Mold or White Plaster Mold on the surface of a bed, before casing. Upper Right: Brown Plaster Mold at same period, showing white mycelium surrounding brown patch of mature mold. Lower: Typical ring of fruiting bodies of Truffle disease on a fine mushroom bed; the mushroom spawn has all been killed within the circle, which is rapidly enlarging. Photograph of Truffle disease loaned by the U. S. Department of Agriculture.

7

produce mushrooms, even when the spawn lower down is vigorous. This dangerous organism is thought to be carried by the small flies that go from older crops to newer fillings. The danger of its attacks is reduced by 1. Keeping the bed surfaces dry before casing so that the spores will not germinate. 2. Keeping down insects. 3. Filling the whole plant nearly at once, to prevent early houses from infecting the later ones. No method of control of this mold is known, once it appears on the beds. Immediate removal of infected compost and replacement with dry soil, may be tried. In worst cases, turning the compost upside down in large chunks, and then casing with dry soil, may make it possible to get part of the crop.

Many harmless molds can be found in the beds and on the surface before the spawn fills the beds. Some of these grow thickly on the surface, especially after sulphur fumigation of the heated house for insect control, but seem to do no harm. But it is possible that this group contains organisms capable of interfering with the crop under special conditions. If any growers suspect this to have occurred they should send samples to a laboratory for study.

The "Truffle", *Pseudobalsamia microspora* Diehl and Lambert, a very serious menace to crops, is an organism still poorly understood.* It is found in large sections of the beds, which will be thickly filled by its small shapeless white fruiting bodies. These are often convoluted, for which it is called the "Calf-brain" disease. They appear on the casing soil as flat white flakes resembling the first mushroom "pinheads." The truffle is found in wet seasons rather than dry, and in long-stored manure, or in compost from wet turning grounds. But once established it returns to the same houses each year, even in dry seasons, with increasing damage. Nothing can be done for it in the beds, but it is wise to remove every trace of it whenever found, taking compost and all, and keeping the compost wet to prevent scattering of the spores. Growers suspecting any growth on their beds to be this organism should send samples to the laboratory. We are confident that control measures will soon be developed.

One or more species of *Trichoderma* and *Penicillium*, common bluish green molds of the soil, may be found in any productive mushroom house if the temperature is kept above 56°F. Small circular patches appear on the soil, growing where mushrooms have been thick, feeding on the dead supporting "roots" left by

* LAMBERT, E. B., Mycologia, 22; 223-226, 1930.

the mushrooms. Such patches should be taken out with the soil beneath, and the gap filled in with new soil. Mushrooms can not grow through this mold. The soil containing it seems to be very toxic. The mold attacks mushrooms at any point where tissues are injured. Bad cases are due to carelessness in removal of dead mushrooms and tissue in the soil, or too hot weather. It is believed that acid soils develop it more quickly than soils neutralized with lime. Severe cases of these molds may develop where mushroom production is entirely stopped. If the spawn is in good condition, and infection of *Mycogone* (see page 53) is not heavy, the soil may then be removed (take along about one-half inch of the compost) and the beds recased.

Olive green mold, *Chaetomium olivaceum* C. and E., is a cellulose-destroying organism which attacks the straw remnants in under-composted manures, appearing two or three weeks after spawning. It has a thin mycelium which is almost invisible, but the fruiting bodies are large enough to be seen with the naked eye, shaped and colored like green olives. It is found in composts which are too "green", too wet, and which have heated over 140° F. in the beds after filling. Infected beds should be given extra ventilation, and watering should be delayed after casing until the spawn has overcome the mold.

In addition to the *Chaetomium* there are several other molds as yet unidentified which often become very dense in composts which are not composted sufficiently. These affect the spawn in the same way, hindering and in some cases stopping its growth.

PARASITIC FUNGI AND DISEASES, WEED FUNGI, MUSHROOM AND SPAWN CONDITIONS

As has already been explained, some of the fungi that invade a mushroom bed attack the mushrooms and ruin their market value. Others attack the spawn. Both these types are known as *Parasitic fungi*.

Weed fungi, on the other hand, live side by side with the mushrooms in the compost, and compete for the available food.

Mushroom and Spawn 'Conditions', however, are not due to the presence of enemy fungi and bacteria, but are brought about by circumstances in the house or in the beds that are not favourable to the proper development of the mushrooms and spawn.

The control of attacks by Parasitic and Weed fungi is made difficult by the fact that the spores of these troubles are widespread in nature and drift into the houses with every breath of fresh air. It would be impossible to maintain a commercial mushroom house in such a state of sterile cleanliness as to exclude these spores entirely. It is difficult to do this, even in a specially designed laboratory.

The most effective means of controlling most of these infections is to prevent the spores from germinating, but before this can be done, the grower must have a knowledge of the various kinds of fungi and bacteria that are liable to attack his crop, and an understanding of the conditions which favour the development of each.

Unfortunately, as new and more effective methods are discovered for controlling and excluding the troubles that we know, the way is thereby left open for other hitherto unknown diseases to develop. Myceliophthora, for instance, is an example of a disease that has only become troublesome within the last ten years—a period during which most of the commoner enemies of the mushroom crop have been routed. Growers who encounter unusual moulds or conditions in their mushroom houses are urged to report the matter without delay to one of the mushroom research stations, for it is only by prompt action that the scientists can hope to find means of controlling these new enemies before they develop into a major menace.

The more commonly encountered diseases and conditions are discussed in detail in this chapter.

[1] Parasitic Fungi

N.B.—With all parasitic infections, it is important to pick off every diseased mushroom before the beds are watered, to avoid washing the disease spores into the soil, where they would infect the pin-head mushrooms.

(a) MYCOGONE PERNICIOSA ('BUBBLES')

Signs of the disease. The pin-head mushrooms are misshapen and develop into distorted lumps covered with a thick, white, thready web. The stem may be bulbous and the gills deformed, or there may be neither cap nor stem, but merely a shapeless, puffy mass. In advanced stages of the disease, the mushrooms ooze drops of amber-coloured liquid and have a putrid smell.

Source of infection. The source of a Mycogone infection is usually the casing soil. Particularly bad infections have been got from soil where wild mushrooms have grown, or where spent mushroom compost has been thrown. If the disease develops with sterilized casing soil, then either the sterilizing was not properly carried out, or the spores must have been present in the manure and escaped destruction during the sweat-out. Other possible sources of infection are (i) carelessly cleaned houses, (ii) airborne infections, (iii) spores carried by insects, (iv) contaminated tools, wheelbarrows, baskets, workers' boots, etc.

Development. The germination of *Mycogone* spores is encouraged by:

(i) High temperatures after casing. The temperature should not be allowed to rise above 68° F. after casing, or over 62° F. during picking, if the spores are suspected of being present.

(ii) Excessive moisture and humidity. Instead of occasional heavy waterings, it is better to water the beds frequently, but lightly. Humidity must be controlled by ventilation.

(iii) Careless trashing. Trash left in the beds after picking is as good as an invitation to 'Bubbles' trouble. Meticulous daily trashing removes these breeding-grounds.

(iv) Poor ventilation. Although not the cause of 'Bubbles', poor ventilation encourages the disease once it has gained a foothold.

Prevention. If possible, the soil to be used should be tested out on a few trial beds the previous year, and, if found to be infected, it can then be sterilized either chemically, or by steam. Houses which have contained contaminated beds must be especially thoroughly cleaned, sprayed, and steamed or fumigated, before another crop is put into them. Any spores that come in with the manure in the new crop will be destroyed during the sweat-out, because a temperature of 110°F. for six hours will kill them.

Cure. The disease, once it has developed, can be retarded by:

(i) Dropping the temperature to 52°F.

(ii) Picking off all infected mushrooms immediately they appear, wrapping them in clean paper to prevent their shedding disease spores on the journey from the bed to the incinerator, and burning them without delay.

(iii) Thorough trashing after picking.

(iv) Giving plenty of fresh air, without chilling the beds.

(v) Spraying the beds between flushes with a dilute Bordeaux solution (2 lb. copper sulphate, 2 lb. hydrated lime/50 gals. water).

(vi) A bushel of screened casing soil mixed with half a pint of formaldehyde per 300 to 400 sq. ft. of bed space can be spread over the beds between flushes. This injures any mushrooms which are on the beds and delays the next flush, but usually frees the crop from *Mycogone*.

If these methods bring no improvement, the casing soil on the beds can be treated.

First pick off all mushrooms and withhold water for from ten to fourteen days till the beds dry out. They should then be sprayed with a 2 per cent formalin solution, allowing about 10 gals. solution/60 ft. of bed. After treatment, the temperature is raised to 65°F., and the beds are left till all traces of the formaldehyde fumes have vanished. The house is then watered back into production. Mushrooms are slow in coming after this treatment, but are usually free from disease when they finally do appear.

Some growers do not dry out the beds before treatment, as they say that the formalin solution is absorbed more readily if the soil is moist.

A speedier remedy that can be tried is to scrape off all the casing soil and re-case with uninfected soil. Those who have tried this are not enthusiastic. Theoretically, a normal crop should follow in about three weeks, but apparently it seldom does.

Control. The surface of a mushroom that is infected by *Mycogone* is covered with thousands of microscopic spores, and anything that comes in contact with an infected mushroom is liable to spread the disease. Shoes, tools, baskets, hands, etc., should all be disinfected with a 4 per cent formalin solution (4 gals. formalin/100 gals. water) or 1 oz. H.T.H. in 5 gals. water.

(b) VERTICILLIUM (BROWN SPOT, FUNGUS SPOT, DRY BUBBLES)

Signs of the disease. The first sign of trouble is the appearance of tiny brown specks on the surface of the mushrooms. These specks gradually become larger, and may become indented, or even deepen into a hole. The stalks of infected mushrooms usually bend or split. Pin-heads, instead of maturing, may grow into small dry puff-balls. At a later stage of the disease, the mushrooms turn dry and leathery, and their caps have a greyish tinge, which is caused by the presence of a multitude of disease spores. The diseased mushrooms should at all costs be removed from the beds before this greyish colour becomes apparent. Otherwise, the spores will be broadcast through the house and it will be a prodigious task to bring the disease under control.

Verticillium can be distinguished from *Mycogone* by the fact that mushrooms affected with *Verticillium* never weep drops of liquid, and have no unpleasant smell.

Source of infection. A *Verticillium* infection usually comes from casing soil, but the spores may be airborne, or brought in by insects, or by workers' boots, etc. They may also be left over from a previous crop, or be present in the manure and escape destruction during a poor sweat-out.

Development. Any conditions adverse to the mushrooms encourage the disease, and the precautions recommended for the control of *Mycogone* are equally effective against *Verticillium*. *Verticillium*, however, spreads more rapidly than any other mushroom disease, and it is imperative to take very active measures against it as soon as it makes an appearance.

Hot humid weather or sudden temperature changes that cause condensation are particularly likely to bring on an attack, as the spores, if present at all, can germinate within a few hours on a damp mushroom cap.

Prevention. Trash the beds thoroughly after each picking and ventilate the house carefully after every watering, or during humid weather, to dry off the mushroom caps. Ensure a good sweat-out to destroy any spores present in the house, or in the manure, and use sterilized or pre-tested casing soil. The spores are killed by a temperature of 104°F. maintained for six hours.

Cure. Bordeaux mixture, sprayed on the beds between flushes, has not been found to be as effective against *Verticillium* as against *Mycogone*, but the new dithiocarbamate dusts give remarkably good results.

Re-casing is not always a successful remedy, but it is sometimes tried if the outbreak of disease is especially bad.

(*c*) BACTERIAL SPOT, PIT, AND BLOTCH

Signs of the disease. (i) *Bacterial Spot.* Pale yellow spots, which appear on the caps of the mushrooms and gradually turn brown can be observed. As the disease progresses, smooth shiny brown streaks may develop at the rim of the cap and converge towards the top of the cap.

(ii) *Pit.* Pin-holes appear in the caps and gradually increase in size and become filled with glistening white pus.

(iii) *Blotch.* This begins as a yellow stain, which gradually turns brown and may spread over the whole surface of the cap. Infected areas are depressed, but discoloration is on the outside only.

Source of infection. There are two distinct schools of thought as to the cause of *Bacterial Pit.* One theory is that the holes are caused by mites—an idea that is supported by the fact that mites are indeed found in the slimy pus filling the holes. The other theory is that the spots are caused by bacteria, which grow on the surface of the mushroom caps, and that the mites are attracted by the pus. Whatever the cause, soils high in organic matter give crops that are particularly prone to develop this trouble.

Bacterial Blotch is encountered most frequently on crops that are grown in caves, and eelworms, which frequently infect the earthy floors of caves, are suspected of carrying the bacteria which cause *Blotch.* These bacteria thrive at low temperatures (52°F. to 55°F.).

Prevention. Those in favour of the 'mite' theory as the cause of 'Pit', believe that the mites are brought in with the soil, and that precautions such as are taken against *Mycogone* and *Verticillium* will exterminate the pests and prevent the disease. Those who support the 'bacteria' theory believe that '*Spot*', 'Pit', and 'Blotch' should all be dealt with in the same way—i.e. by keeping the mushroom caps dry, because bacteria can only develop on a moist surface.

Fans can be used to keep the air circulating and prevent excessive humidity. As with all mushroom diseases, any conditions adverse to the mushrooms encourage these troubles.

Cure. Dusting the surface of the soil thinly and evenly with one part hydrated lime to one part soil is said to have brought good results in several instances, but the grower is advised to experiment with this treatment on a small area of bed space before trying it wholesale, as it may not be suitable for the casing soil in use.

Alternatively, the methods recommended for dealing with *Mycogone* infections can be tried.

Treatment for Mite infestations is outlined in Chapter Twelve.

(*d*) TRICHODERMA (BLOTCH)

Signs of the disease. The fungus and spores of this disease are green, but they cause a dark brown, irregularly shaped blotch to appear on the surface of the caps of affected mushrooms. Underneath this discoloured patch, the flesh of the mushroom rots away. The stems have black streaks running down them, and they sometimes split as with *Verticillium*.

Cause. High temperatures, high humidity, wet mushroom caps.

Development. Unfavourable conditions.

Prevention and cure. Keep the mushroom caps dry. This disease rarely becomes widespread.

(*e*) FLOCK OR GILL MOULD; OPEN VEIL

Signs of the disease. Little is known about 'Flock' and 'Open Veil', and it has not yet been definitely established whether they are the same disease, or two different diseases. With '*Flock*', the gills of affected mushrooms are joined together and covered with a white mould. The veil is always broken and the cap and gills are hard. With '*Open Veil*', the mushrooms develop with no veils, or partly formed veils, and in cases where the trouble is severe and widespread, the mushrooms are small, hard, and leathery, with white, tough, undeveloped gills. Even slightly affected mushrooms lose their market value. The trouble may appear only here and there on the bed, or may affect the whole crop. It has been known to appear in one flush only, or in every flush.

Cause. The cause is unknown. The suggestion that some strains of spawn give crops that are prone to develop these troubles has never been either substantiated or disproved.

Prevention and cure. It is impossible to prevent a disease occurring, if the cause is not known, and it is equally difficult to cure it. The accepted treatment is to pick off all affected mushrooms as they appear. Severe outbreaks have been brought under control in a few cases by drying off the beds for a short while, and then watering them back into production. Since this is the only remedy so far devised, it is worth a trial. Fortunately, the trouble is not common. Research may yield a solution shortly.

(*f*) FUSARIUM (DAMPING OFF)

Signs of the disease. Affected mushrooms look perfectly normal in the early stages of the disease, and it may be only when they are picked that they are discovered to be withered and pithy, with the inside of the stem turned brown. The trouble starts with a few patches of infected mushrooms here and there on the beds, but, if unchecked, it soon spreads through the crop. Once the disease gains a foothold, its presence is more easily detected, for the mushroom caps have an unnatural, polished appearance, and are darker in colour than those of healthy mushrooms. In really bad infections, the mushrooms do not develop beyond the button stage and have a lop-sided, mummified look. If left on the beds, they will last for months without decaying. White mushrooms are more susceptible to *Fusarium* than brown ones are.

Source of infection. Opinions are divided. Most growers blame the start of the disease on infected casing soil, but a few insist that, like other mushroom diseases, it is brought on by unsuitable conditions, such as over-wet soil, or soil which cakes or is non-porous, or any other condition that cuts off the air supply from the compost.

Prevention. Sterilize the casing soil and maintain conditions favourable to mushroom growth.

Cure. Isolated patches of infected mushrooms should be treated without delay with a mixture of eleven parts ammonium carbonate to one part copper sulphate, every ½ oz. of the mixture being diluted with $\frac{1}{2}$ gal. of water. This prevents the disease spreading, and if, after this, it continues to appear, then the infection must be widespread through the casing soil, which must be scraped off and replaced with sterilized, pre-tested soil.

(g) MUMMY DISEASE

Signs of the disease. Pin-heads fail to mature, and infected mushrooms become dry and leathery and will not decay. The stems swell at the base, and are bent and distorted. The flesh of the mushroom is full of soft pus or streaks. The infection may be restricted to isolated patches, or to a few beds only. Usually, the trouble does not make its appearance until the later flushes.

Cause. Unknown, but it is believed to be due to a virus.

Cure. Do everything possible to prevent the trouble from spreading. Treat the infected spots as soon as they appear. The most successful treatment so far discovered is to dig a trench about 1 ft. wide on either side of the infected area at a distance of 6 ft. from it. A 2 per cent formalin solution is then sprayed over the infected part at the rate of 1 gal. per 6 ft. of bed space.

Prevention. Maintain good conditions. Use sterilized casing soil.

(h) DACTYLIUM (MILDEW)

Signs of the disease. A silky white growth that develops a granulated appearance with age, spreads over the surface of the soil and mushrooms, like a cobweb or veil. The mushrooms become shrunken, decompose, and topple over on the bed, where they are finally completely cocooned in white mould mycelium. Usually this trouble only develops in the later flushes.

Source of infection. The source of the trouble is believed to be the casing soil, and development is encouraged by high humidity and excessive moisture.

Development. The disease spreads rapidly and steps should be taken to control it as soon as it appears.

Prevention. Pre-test the casing soil and sterilize it if it is found to be infected. Control moisture and humidity during cropping.

Cure. Soak the affected spots with a 15 per cent formaldehyde solution (1 gal. formalin per 7 gals. water). Sterilize tools, etc., to prevent the disease spreading.

[2] Weed Fungi

(a) TRUFFLE (CALVES' BRAINS)

Signs of the disease. The first sign of truffle is the appearance of the truffle mycelium in the manure. It looks like wefts or streaks of white cotton, and is usually first observed on the surface of the casing soil or under the side-boards. The mycelium becomes thicker and develops into small, crinkly bodies about the size of pin-head mushrooms, which is what inexperienced growers usually imagine them to be. As the bodies mature, they turn brown and decay. In bad infections, these truffle 'bodies' are found, not only on the surface of the beds, but also throughout the soil and manure. In such cases, the mushroom spawn becomes a wet, pulpy mass and the beds have a strong disagreeable smell like chlorine. Outbreaks of truffle are usually most severe during hot weather.

Source of infection. The spores are usually got from the casing soil, but they are sometimes picked up by manure composted on grass-land, instead of the usual cement- or cinder-based composting ground. Infection may also be got from yards where the surrounding land drains down on to the composting manure. The mixing of soil into the manure during composting has been blamed for several outbreaks and this is one of the main reasons why this practice has been abandoned.

Once the disease has been introduced into the house, the most dangerous source of infection is the house itself.

Truffle is now believed to be a parasitic fungus that lives on the mushroom mycelium. If true, this may account for the wet, soggy condition of the spawn in affected mushroom beds. The theory is further borne out by the odd fact that even when truffle spores are known to be present in the manure, and conditions of temperature and moisture are favourable for their germination, the truffle will not start to grow until the beds are spawned.

Development. Truffle spores germinate best at 83° F., but at 70° F., the temperature at which the beds are usually spawned, they germinate and produce fruiting bodies within three weeks. They will not germinate at either temperature, however, unless mushroom mycelium is present in the beds. At 60° F., they do not germinate at all, even if the spawn is running well, and this gives the grower an infallible method of preventing the germination of the truffle spores, since all he has to do is to delay spawning till the temperature reaches 60° F.

Unfortunately, 'low-temperature spawning' does not give complete control, for truffle mycelium grows vigorously at 60° F., so that if there are any traces of truffle mycelium in the bed-boards, these will grow into the manure as soon as the spawn starts running.

A third danger is that if the truffle spores are present in the house, a spell of hot weather may force the bed temperature high enough to allow them to germinate. If the spores are present in great numbers and widespread through the house, a total crop failure may result.

Truffle is a freakish, unpredictable disease, for sometimes, even when the spores are known to be present during the spawn run and conditions are favourable for their germination, the disease un-accountably fails to make an appearance. Test beds, deliberately infected with truffle spores, have not developed the disease, in spite of sustained efforts to encourage it, but truffle mycelium, dug up out of infected beds and replanted, grows vigorously and develops many fruiting bodies, which produce a multitude of fresh spores.

Prevention. Truffle spores are extremely difficult to destroy. They survive temperatures of 160° F. maintained for five hours, and are completely unaffected by any of the disinfectants and fumigants in regular use. The temperature of boiling water, maintained for two hours, will kill them, but since the house and compost cannot be boiled, this information is not of much use to the grower.

Small articles, such as tools, buckets, or even infected bed-boards might, of course, be treated in this way, provided a large enough tank was available to boil them in.

Truffle spores in the soil survive all the usual methods of soil sterilization, and attempts to eliminate them by mixing formaldehyde into the water in the steam boiler have so far proved to have a very damaging effect on most soils, but little or no effect on the truffle spores. At present, the only way to avoid introducing truffle spores with the casing soil is to pre-test the soil and make sure that it is free of them.

Fortunately, truffle mycelium is more easily got rid of. It can be destroyed by ensuring a good sweat-out, by thorough cleaning, disinfecting and, if possible, steam pasteurizing of houses that have borne infected crops, and by normal methods of soil sterilization.

Some growers say that wet manure encourages the disease, while others insist that infections are worse when the manure is on the dry side. All agree that high temperatures, poor ventilation, and beds into which air cannot penetrate aggravate the trouble.

Cure. Once truffle is discovered in the beds, treatment must be directed towards (i) preventing the mycelium from running any further through the compost; (ii) destroying the fruiting bodies before they have time to bear spores.

Soaking the truffle mycelium with a disinfectant solution appears to have little effect on the mycelium and none on the spores. If the infected patches are small, they can be dug up and burnt, along with a good part of the surrounding manure. Especial care must be taken when removing the diseased compost from the house, for fragments of truffle mycelium dropped inadvertently on neighbouring beds would start to grow and set up a new infection. Tools, and buckets used during the removal should be boiled. None of the infected compost should be put into baskets or barrows that are to be used for the next crop, and none of it should be thrown negligently on a trash heap or on nearby land.

If a very large portion of the bed is infected it should be isolated by digging a wide trench right across the bed on either side of the diseased area, which must thereafter be allowed to dry out completely. When the house is emptied, this area should be removed first and burnt, and the bed-boards that have been in contact with it must receive extra special treatment. Some growers burn the bed-boards too.

If the disease is widespread throughout the house, little can be done, except to dry out the house as quickly as possible, dispose of the infected compost in the safest way that can be devised, and employ every means available to clean the house before another crop is put into it. Normally, outbreaks severe enough to cause a total crop failure only occur during hot weather, and are not likely to develop even then, unless there is a very strong concentration of spores in the house, the manure, or the casing soil.

Precautions

  (i) Pre-test all casing soil.

  (ii) Do not mix soil into the compost.

  (iii) Compost on a hard-packed, properly drained composting yard.

  (iv) If truffle spores are thought to be present in the house or manure, run the crop at 60° F. at the highest. At this temperature, the spawn growth will be slow, but should be free from disease. Most growers plant twice the usual amount of spawn to get the beds impregnated with mycelium faster.

(b) BROWN PLASTER MOULD

Signs of the disease. A dense white patch about 6 to 8 in. in diameter appears on the surface of the beds, either on the manure before casing, or on the casing soil. As the mould develops, a yellow tinge begins at the centre and gradually spreads over the whole patch until only the fringe of it remains white. The yellow colour deepens into brown and takes on a granulated appearance, which is caused by masses of tiny solid bodies called 'bulbils'. This is a dormant stage.

Source of infection. Improperly composted manure, wet compost, chilling of the beds, temperature fluctuations, poor ventilation.

Development. The mould is rarely widespread and does little damage, except when conditions are very bad, in which case the crop will be poor anyway, even without the mould. While the patch remains white, it prevents the growth of mushroom spawn, but once it turns brown, mushrooms will actually grow through the mould, though not as plentifully as in the unaffected parts of the beds.

Prevention. Cleanliness, i.e. proper decontamination of the composting yard, houses, tools, lorries, etc., after each crop. Maintenance of good conditions, i.e. satisfactory fermentation of manure, control of ventilation, temperature, and moisture. All these precautions help to reduce the risk of the mould developing.

Cure. Once the mould has developed, all that can be done is to remedy the unfavourable conditions as far as possible, and wait for the mould to turn brown.

(c) WHITE PLASTER MOULD (FLOUR MOULD)

Signs of the disease. Patches of chalky-white powdery growth on the top of the beds, either on the surface of the manure before casing, or on the soil surface after casing. This mould can be distinguished from Brown Plaster Mould by the fact that the patches do not change colour as they develop, beyond taking on a slightly pinkish tinge in the later stages. It is considered to be a more serious disease than the Brown Mould, because mushrooms seldom grow on the affected spots. Fortunately, the outbreak is rarely widespread enough to cause much reduction in the crop.

Source of infection. The mould usually appears on green, very alkaline manure, or on badly fermented manure. It sometimes develops on beds that have been chilled or over-watered.

Development. Poor ventilation and excessive moisture encourage the mould. The spores are always present in the air, ready to invade the beds at the first favourable moment.

Prevention. Maintain good conditions and see that the manure is properly composted.

Cure. None has so far been discovered, but when conditions improve, the patches sometimes disappear of their own accord.

(d) GREEN MOULD

Signs of the disease. A dark green patch of mould with a rough, granulated appearance develops on top of the casing soil, especially round butts or trash left on the beds.

Source of infection. This mould flourishes on decayed organic matter, such as dead spawn, butts, trash, under-composted plant material, etc., and is encouraged by warm, wet, acid conditions in the soil.

Development. No mushrooms will grow on the affected parts of the bed.

Prevention. Take care that all organic matter in the casing soil is thoroughly decomposed before the soil is put on the beds. Trash meticulously after every picking, and fill the holes with a mixture of one part hydrated lime to twenty parts of screened casing soil. This should prevent sour conditions developing. Guard against over-watering and keep the temperature down.

Cure. Remove the mouldy parts of the bed with a trowel, and take some of the surrounding soil along with the diseased parts. The holes should then be filled up with the lime and soil mixture. If the disease shows signs of becoming widespread, the surface of the bed can be broadcasted with a mixture of 1 part lime/10 parts soil.

(e) CHAETOMIUM (OLIVE-GREEN MOULD)

Signs of the disease. A fine grey mycelium appears in the casing soil about a week after spawning. Usually, this is not noticed, although it retards the growth of the mushroom mycelium. Fruiting bodies

PLATE 17

Olive-green mould (Chaetomium)

Truffle on casing soil

Vert de gris on manure

Dactylium deuderoides (Mildew)

PLATE 18

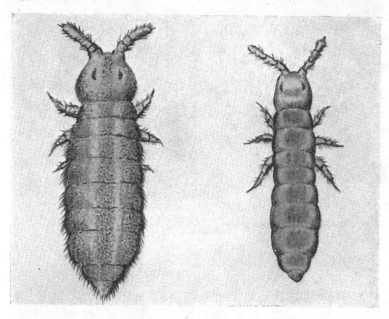

*Springtails
enlarged*

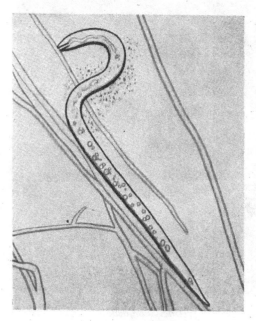

*A Nematode
very much
enlarged*

develop about two weeks after spawning. These are small olive-green balls of mould which form abundantly, especially on the straw in the manure. Sometimes, the whole compost is smothered in them, but, since the 'bodies' are very small, a close scrutiny is needed before they are observed. Diseased beds have a musty odour.

Cause. The mould develops in manure that has been damaged by overheating during the sweat-out, i.e. temperatures above 145° F. It is believed that the spores are always present in the manure, but are only able to germinate in overheated compost. If the manure was originally under-composted and very alkaline, it is particularly prone to suffer from this disease.

Development. Mushroom spawn growth is retarded. Mushroom production is usually very poor, though this may be due as much to the damaged condition of the manure as to the presence of the mould.

Prevention. Do not allow the beds to overheat during the sweat-out.

Cure. None known, but ventilation helps the condition. Some growers remove the side-boards to let the air get at the compost.

(f) MYXOMYCETES (SLIME MOULD)

Signs of the disease. Slimy, mouldy, wet spots appear on the surface of the beds. Where mushrooms are grown on shelves, thick slimy matter may drip from the upper beds on to the shelves below.

Predisposing factor. The mould is liable to develop on excessively wet spots on the beds.

Development. The mould is rarely widespread throughout the crop, and if it is, the beds must already have been in such a sodden condition as to make cropping highly unlikely.

Prevention and cure. Do not over-water the beds.

(g) MYCELIOPHTHORA (MAT DISEASE, VERT DE GRIS)

Signs of the disease. This is a disease that has only become troublesome in the last decade, and little is known about it. The first evidence that anything is amiss is that apparently normal beds cease to bear mushrooms. Investigation shows that a corky brown crust has developed between the compost and the soil. Within the crust, there are small brown fruiting bodies, filled with glistening dark brown cells, but these generally pass unnoticed. The crust grows

M

over the surface of the manure like a mat and forms a layer between the compost and casing soil through which the spawn is unable to penetrate. Consequently, there is no crop. The spawn growth below the mat appears perfectly healthy. In the early stages of the disease, which are not normally observed, a thick white felty mycelium grows between the soil and compost. As this mycelium thickens into a mat, the colour turns gradually to a yellowish brown.

Source of infection. It is generally agreed that 'Mat' disease is due to the presence of Myceliophthora spores in the casing soil.

Prevention and cure. The spores are very difficult to eradicate, because they survive temperatures of 165° F. and most of the chemical methods of soil sterilization. Once the disease has occurred in a house, it is apt to attack each succeeding crop with increasing virulence. Attempts have been made to sterilize both soil and infected houses with a combination of steam and formaldehyde. (For soil, add 1 to 2 gals. formaldehyde to every 100 gals. water in the steam boiler. For houses, vaporize 2 to 4 gals. formaldehyde in each house during steaming. Steam for six hours.) The value of this treatment is uncertain, and the soil is apt to be so badly damaged that the resultant crop reduction is worse than that caused by the 'Mat' disease.

It is hoped that a satisfactory method of dealing with the disease will be found soon. The temperature of the beds during cropping does not appear to have any effect, adverse or otherwise, on the development of the disease.

(*h*) SPOROTRICHUM

(*Note.*—Opinions are divided as to whether *Sporotrichum* and *Myceliophthora* are two different diseases, or one and the same disease in different forms. Those who favour the second theory believe that 'Mat' disease is due to the presence of the Myceliophthora spores in the casing soil, whereas the condition to be described as Sporotrichum is the result of the Myceliophthora spores being present in the compost. At the moment, so little is known about either condition that it would be pointless to take sides in the controversy.

Whatever the cause, the two conditions are distinctive in form, but similar in effect, for both can cause a complete crop failure.)

Signs of the disease. No mat forms between the compost and soil.

Instead, the manure is filled with blobs, streaks, and sheets of yellowish mould. The mushroom spawn may disappear completely as the mould develops, but the compost does not turn black and sodden, as with Truffle infections.

Source of infection. Whether or not this condition is due to the presence of Myceliophthora spores in the manure, it appears to be connected with manure from places such as race-tracks, where sour, musty fermentation is liable to have taken place, or with over-wet manure into which musty hay or straw has been mixed, or with manure that has been composted where surrounding land could drain down on to it, or manure through which soil has been mixed, either purposely or inadvertently.

All these conditions are easily avoided, and this may be the reason why this form of infection is less common than 'Mat' disease.

Cure. If the compost is thought to be infected, some growers let the temperature of the manure rise to 168° F. for six hours during peak heat, then attempt to compensate for the overheating by holding the beds at 130° F. for about four days thereafter. This is a risky and unorthodox stratagem of no very certain effectiveness, but it is given because it is the only treatment so far devised.

(*i*) INK CAPS (FALSE MUSHROOMS)

Signs of the disease. Ink caps usually appear on the surface of the manure before the beds are cased. They are easily distinguished from genuine mushrooms by their long spindly stalks and small umbrella-like caps. The gills turn black and ooze drops of black liquid. Often, the cap splits, the splits running from the edge to the centre of the cap. Even if these Ink Caps should be eaten in error, there would no ill consequences, as they are edible, though not palatable.

Predisposing factor. The presence of a large crop of Ink Caps is usually taken as in indication that the manure is rather green and too wet.

Development. Ink Caps are seldom troublesome and rarely appear in more than isolated patches.

Prevention. Longer composting; drier compost.

Cure. Although the Ink Caps usually do no harm, they should be picked off as they appear, as, if left to rot on the beds, they may cause moulds.

(*j*) CUP FUNGI (PEZIZA SP.)

Signs of the disease. Small black, yellow, or brown rubbery-looking fruiting bodies shaped like cups appear on the surface of the beds.

Source of infection. Their presence is usually an indication that the manure has been badly composted. Heat encourages their development.

Prevention. Compost carefully. Avoid high temperatures after casing.

Cure. Pick off the fruiting bodies as they appear and dig out the butts.

(*k*) XYLARIA VAPORARIA

Signs of the disease. This fungus weed grows from a coarse white mycelium and forms fruiting bodies about 4 in. long and up to $1\frac{1}{2}$ in. wide. These look like pieces of twisted root and are white at first, but eventually turn black. Treat as for Cup Fungi.

(*l*) CAT'S EAR FUNGUS (CLITEFULAS CRETATUS)

Description. Small patches of white shell-shaped fruiting bodies, rather like cat's ears appear on the surface of the casing soil. These 'ears' grow on short stems and have white gills on the underside. They develop from a thin white mycelium. Usually there are only a few isolated patches and the trouble is regarded as one of minor importance.

Source of infection. The spores of the fungus are usually brought in with the soil and are especially likely to be found in soil from the neighbourhood of a wood, or soil that has been contaminated by decayed wood.

Prevention. Pre-test soil and sterilize if necessary.

Cure. Pick off the fruiting bodies as they appear.

[3] Mushroom Conditions

(*a*) ROSE-COMB

Description. The caps of the mushrooms become distorted and warty, with patches of irregular, leathery gills forming growths on their surfaces.

Cause. This condition is due to the presence in the mushroom house of mineral oils such as paraffin or coal oil. The distortion of the mushroom caps is induced by the vapour given off. Sometimes the condition appears when no oil is present and cannot be accounted for.

Prevention. Never use mineral oil in lamps or heaters for the mushroom houses. Never use preparations that contain these oils for spraying the beds, keeping down flies, or sterilizing houses, tools, and bed-boards.

Cure. Once the cause of the trouble has been discovered and removed, the condition usually disappears of its own accord.

(b) CARBON DIOXIDE INJURY (MADER'S THEORY)

Signs of the trouble. The mushrooms develop with long thin stems and small dwarf caps. The button mushrooms are very small.

Cause. At one time it was thought that this condition was due to an accumulation of carbon dioxide in the mushroom house as a result of poor ventilation, but Dr. Lambert has shown that while a concentration of as little as 2 per cent of carbon dioxide does have a harmful effect on the crop, conditions in affected houses rarely prove to have a carbon dioxide concentration strong enough to account for the amount of injury that has developed. It has also been shown that mushrooms in caves sometimes develop this condition, even when there is no concentration of carbon dioxide at all.

Dr. Mader, after considerable experimenting and investigation, came to the conclusion that the growing mushrooms give off a toxic gas, and that if the gas is not removed by adequate ventilation, the accumulation of gas induces a form of self-poisoning. This theory has been confirmed by the experiments of Dr. Sinden.

Cure. Ventilation must be adjusted so as to give a continuous supply of fresh air during cropping, the amount required depending on the amount of bed space that is packed into the cubic capacity of the house. (Three to seven air changes per hour.) Air movement must be ensured by the use of strategically placed fans, so that every part of the house gets a fair share of the available fresh air. There must be no pools of stagnant air in odd corners or over and around the bottom beds.

Dr. Sinden found that the accumulation of gas could be cured by introducing a substance such as activated charcoal to absorb it, but this idea has not been developed commercially.

(c) STROMA

This is not a mushroom disease, but a condition of the spawn. The mycelium threads on the surface of the casing soil fluff up like cotton wool and will not form pin-heads. This happens when the casing soil is dry underneath and moist on the surface.

Remedy. Water the beds adequately and ventilate well. Make sure that the humidity in the house is not excessive.

Where the Stroma is very thick, it may be necessary to rake over the surface with a small hand fork before the water can penetrate through the spawn fluff to the soil beneath.

Once the condition is cured, a normal crop follows. So far, no reduction in the cropping capacity of the bed has been reported to have resulted from the development of a Stroma condition.

(d) CHEMICAL INJURY

This condition may take a multitude of forms. The mushrooms may be distorted or discoloured; pin-heads may 'mat', instead of forming into mushrooms; the spawn may refuse to run, or may become thickened and rope-like. Any of these conditions may be due to injury caused by some chemical that has been used in the mushroom house or during the sterilization of the soil. Consequently new brands of insecticide or fungicide, or new methods of sterilizing the house or the soil should be tried out cautiously on a small scale first, before being used with a lavish hand.

THE TRUFFLE DISEASE OF CULTIVATED MUSHROOMS

by EDMUND B. LAMBERT

Reprinted from Circular Letter of the U. S. DEPT. OF AGRICULTURE, July, 1932.

SYMPTOMS.

The disease usually becomes apparent in the beds at about the time the casing soil is applied. Oftentimes two or three normal breaks of mushrooms appear on affected beds before the disease develops. Usually it appears first as fungus wefts under the side-boards. These wefts are cream-colored, cottony growths about one-half to two inches in diameter. After 5 or 6 days they become rounded up into firm wrinkled fungus tissue, resembling small calves' brains. In this condition they are often mistaken for deformed or rudimentary mushrooms. These structures are the fruiting bodies of the fungus causing the disease. After they begin to form, similar fruiting bodies can usually be found throughout the compost as shown in figure 1. A few days later they may appear over the surface of the soil where they often form "fairy rings" 4 or 5 feet in diameter as they spread out from centers of infestation. The appearance of the fungus on the soil in most cases marks the end of the crop in the infested area, as shown in figure 2. A few weeks later the mycelium of both the truffle and mushroom disappears from the compost. Infested houses have a distinct odor which although difficult to describe is easily recognized when it has once been encountered. As a rule beds of the white variety are more severely infested than those of the brown variety.

THE TRUFFLE FUNGUS

The truffle disease was so named because the fungus causing it (*Pseudobalsamia microspora*) is classified in the same general group as the truffle of commerce. This fungus seems to act like a weed in the bed rather than a parasite and during the early run of the mushroom spawn it appears to stimulate the mushroom mycelium rather than retard it. The spores are borne inside of the fruiting body and are liberated only when the fruiting bodies disintegrate. Very little is known regarding the factors affecting the longevity or germination of the spores, the growth of the mycelium, or the production of fruiting bodies.

PROBABLE MEANS OF DISSEMINATION

The source of this fungus is not known since it has never been found outside of mushroom houses. There are two types of infestation that must be considered, (1) the initial infestation, which is often confined to a few small areas on the bed, and (2) the re-infestation which frequently involves an entire house or several houses.

The fact that the disease is so widespread indicates that the truffle fungus is widespread in nature. The habits of closely related fungi and the history of the disease suggest that it normally lives in the soil. Therefore casing soil, the soil of the composting grounds, manure, storage grounds or soil added to compost are the most likely sources of initial infestation. Spawn may be eliminated from consideration because the disease has appeared simultaneously in the houses of several growers using spawn from entirely different sources. Furthermore, the truffle fungus when grown experimentally in spawn bottles is so conspicuous that it hardly seems possible for it to be distributed in this way without detection.

Once the truffle disease has appeared in a mushroom house, re-infestation usually occurs and frequently the disease becomes increasingly prevalent in subsequent crops. It seems improbable that casing soil has been the source of severe re-infestations because in many instances the fruiting bodies of the truffle fungus developed before the casing soil was applied. Circumstantial evidence indicates that the fungus follows one or more of three courses: Either it lives over from one crop to another inside of the mushroom house; it persists in the soil of the composting grounds; or it develops in soil which is later added to the compost. If it remains in the mushroom house, the fact that it persists in spite of ordinary sulphur or formaldehyde fumigation indicates that the spores can withstand this treatment or that the fungus escapes the fumigant by penetrating deeply in the bed boards. The fact that the disease frequently reappears in subsequent crops in the same spot in the beds points strongly to the theory of fungus penetrating into the bed boards. Spores are probably widely distributed at the time of emptying the beds and many of them undoubtedly are blown onto the composting ground where it is entirely possible that they may remain to reinfest a new compost heap. In test tubes these spores have been shown to be capable of withstanding temperatures of at least 180°F. for 5 hours. Therefore they may easily

32

live through the temperatures generated in the compost heap and in the house during the final fermentation in the bed.

Observation of numerous cases indicates that the disease is aggravated by such conditions as: Poorly drained composting grounds, wet compost, high temperatures during the run of spawn, storing the manure, and the addition of soil or muck to the heap during composting. A clear understanding of these points must await further observation and experiments.

TENTATIVE CONTROL MEASURES.

In view of the foregoing observations it would seem advisable for a grower whose house has been infested with the truffle fungus to take the following precautionary measures: Increase the dosage for fumigating the empty house; disinfect or replace the bed boards; disinfect the composting grounds; see that the composting grounds are well drained; discontinue adding soil or muck to the manure or change the source of the soil added; avoid storing manure; early fall crops; running the spawn at high temperatures; and a wet soggy condition of the compost during the fermentation in the pile or in the house. Some of these measures may prove superfluous in the light of further investigations but it would seem wiser to do too much than too little.

RELATION OF TEMPERATURE TO CONTROL OF MYCOGONE PERNICIOSA.

by EDMUND B. LAMBERT

Reprinted from PHYTOPATHOLOGY, XX., 75-83. Jan. 1930.

RATE OF GROWTH AND INFECTION.

Further experiments were made to determine if infection is diminished by low temperatures. In these experiments twelve mushroom cultures in aluminum cans were cased with artificially-infested moist soil and twelve were cased with Mycogone-free soil as checks. The cans were then placed in rooms in which constant temperatures were maintained at 21° C., 15° C., and 10° C. (70°, 60°, and 50° F.). There was 100 per cent infection in the eight cultures which were infested and held at 21° C. and at 15° C., while, at 10° C., there were more normal than infected mushrooms. There was also only a partial infection in cultures which had been 100 per cent infected at 21° C. and subsequently cleaned of bubbles and placed to grow again at 13° C. and 10° C. . . . These experiments substantiate the observation of the growers that Mycogone is retarded to a greater extent than mushrooms by low temperatures and indicate that, even in the presence of an excess of inoculum, less bubbles may be expected at temperatures approaching 10° C. than at temperatures above 15° C. . . .

EXPERIMENTS WITH HEATED SOIL.

The results of the preceding experiments indicate that even the air temperature in the upper part of a well-managed mushroom house is high enough during the fermentation period to kill Mycogone spores. This suggested the possibility of utilizing this heat to eradicate soil infestation by placing the casing soil inside the mushroom house during the fermentation period. Several experiments were made to determine whether soil could be successfully treated in this way. In one series of tests, artificially-infested soil was subjected to temperatures of 52° C. and 45° C. (126° and 113° F.) for different lengths of time and subsequently used for casing mushroom cultures. The cultures were then placed under ideal conditions for the development of bubbles, the presence or absence of which was used as the criterion of presence or absence of the pathogene in the soil. The results of these tests, given in table 1, substantiate the conclusion drawn from data obtained with pure cultures on agar. Altogether they seemed to warrant making further tests in a commercial mushroom house.

TABLE 1.—*The effect of heating soil which has been artificially infested with Mycogone perniciosa (strains 48, 8, and 13A) on the amount of infection in cultures of Agaricus campestris, in which this soil was used for casing*

Temperature Centigrade	No. of hours treated	Number of mushrooms growing			
		Trial I		Trial II	
		Infected	Healthy	Infected	Healthy
52	Check	6	0	4	0
	6 hours	2	29	0	10
	12 "	0	16	0	1
	24 "	0	10	0	6
45	Check	33	0	4	0
	6 hours	1	11	1	4
	12 "	0	17	0	3
	24 "	0	1	0	22

In these experiments both naturally and artificially infested soils were subjected to the heat generated by fermenting manure.* The soil was placed in round metal pans 5 in. deep by 18 in. in diameter. These pans were set in a mushroom house over fermenting manure, with one edge touching the manure. The temperature of the soil rose to 131° F., about halfway between the air temperature (118° F.) and the manure temperature (140° F.). This temperature was maintained over night, about 14 hours. In the morning the house was opened to release the cyanide gas and the temperature immediately began to fall. By the next morning, when the soil was removed from the house, the temperature of the soil had dropped to 108° F. Four sections of bed were cased with this soil: Two with heated soil, naturally infested and artificially infested, and two with unheated soil, naturally- and artificially infested.

Six weeks later there was 100 per cent infection on the artificially infested check plot and on the naturally infested check plot there was about 80 per cent infection, while on both the plots cased with heated soil there was no trace of infection. The high percentage of infection in the check plot cased with naturally infested soil and the complete absence of infection in the corresponding heated plot were of particular interest since they offer at least once piece of evidence indicating that there are not likely to be more resistant spore forms in nature than there were in our artificially infested cultures.

---

*The naturally infested soil was garden soil, heavily fertilized with spent mushroom manure for three years. The experiments were made in the houses of the Keystone Mushroom Company, Coatesville, Pennsylvania, and the facilities for making them were kindly placed at my disposal by Mr. L. F. Lambert and Mr. Charles H. G. Sweigart.

Discussions and Conclusions

The results of the experiments presented in this paper tend to clear up several phases of the Mycogone problem: They offer a reasonable explanation for the severe outbreaks of bubbles which are so often associated with hot weather, they suggest a method of reducing the loss in infested houses, they indicate that manure probably is not a source of inoculum in mushroom houses in which there is an active fermentation during the final heat, and they suggest a simple and inexpensive method of eradicating *M. perniciosa* from infested casing-soil. The severe infection often appearing in houses which have been overheated during or following a hot spell seems to be due to the fact that the optimum temperature for the growth of *M. perniciosa* is higher than the normal range of temperatures for growing mushrooms, and the comparative scarcity of disease in cool houses seems to be correlated with the fact that under controlled conditions only sporadic infections develop at temperatures approaching 10° C. (50° F.), even in the presence of an abundance of inoculum in the soil. In view of these facts it would seem advisable to keep the temperature below 13° C. (55° F.) in all houses known to be heavily infested.

Mycogone perniciosa has been shown to be quite sensitive to prolonged exposure to moderately high temperature. This indicates that it probably cannot withstand the temperatures developed in manure during active fermentation, especially during the final heat in the mushroom house. If the manure is left out of consideration, there is considerable circumstantial evidence which indicates that casing soil is the principal source of inoculum. Beach (1) came to this conclusion after three years' observation of conditions in Pennsylvania; and Smith (3), in England, and Beach have shown that formaldehyde can be used successfully to eradicate Mycogone from soil. In practice, however, this method has certain obvious disadvantages and it would seem to be simpler, safer, and less expensive for the average commercial grower to eradicate Mycogone from his casing soil by taking advantage of the low thermal death point of this fungus. The experiments outlined above indicate that usually high enough temperatures are generated in mushroom houses while the manure is going through its final heat. Of course, further work must be done before we can be sure that sufficient heat will be generated in all cases and that there are not heat-resistant strains of *M. perniciosa* in the soil. Perhaps it will be necessary to use artificial heat.

FLIES, INSECT PESTS, AND RODENTS

[1] Flies

All fly infestations are dealt with in much the same way, so a brief description of the types of fly pest that the grower is likely to encounter is followed by a discussion of the most up-to-date methods of dealing with the problem.

(a) SCIARID FLIES (FUNGUS GNAT)

Several species are found, all very similar to each other.

Adult flies. Small, slender, dark brown or black antennae; long thin legs; long delicate wings, which fold flat when at rest. Usually, the flies are sluggish, and crawl about the beds or cling to the bedboards.

Eggs. Laid in the manure or casing soil or on the mushrooms; oval; white or yellow; so small that they are not easily seen unless found massed together. One female can lay as many as 300 eggs.

Grubs. Hatch from the eggs in about four to six days; legless white maggots with shiny black heads. The maggots are almost transparent against the light. They grow to about $\frac{1}{4}$ in. in length, shedding their skins periodically during the period of growth, which lasts from ten to fourteen days according to the temperature. At temperatures of 70°F. to 75°F., they grow quickly; below 55°F., they develop more slowly. When fully grown, they spin a silky pupa or cocoon in which they pupate. After five to seven days, they emerge from their cocoons as adult flies and are capable of mating within a few hours. The whole life cycle takes from two to four weeks.

Injury. The grubs feed on the newly planted spawn pieces, on the spawn mycelium, and on the roots of the mushrooms. Occasionally, they chew up the manure, leaving it broken down and blackish in colour. Sometimes they burrow up the stems of the mushrooms and eat tunnels through the caps. Pin-head mushrooms may be completely hollowed out and used as a nest for a colony of grubs. The spawn growth may become thick and stringy.

The market value of the mushrooms which have been attacked is destroyed. The damage to the compost, spawn, and pin-heads causes a severe reduction in crop.

(b) PHORID FLIES (MANURE FLIES)

Several species are found, all very much alike.

Adult flies. Their bodies are shorter and thicker than those of the Sciarid flies. They have smaller heads and larger chests, which gives them a hump-backed look. They are more active on the beds and move in quick, jerky runs.

Eggs. Laid in or on the manure; small, white, oval; scarcely visible to the naked eye; hatch in about six days.

Grubs. Smaller than the Sciarid grubs; shiny, legless, slightly pointed at head and tail; all white or yellow; pupate after about ten days; emerge as adult flies in about fourteen days. Their colouring makes them readily distinguishable from the Sciarid grubs, which have black heads.

Injury. The Phorid maggots cause the same kind of damage as the Sciarid grubs, except that only one species of Phorid grub eats into the mushrooms.

(c) CECID FLIES (GALL GNATS)

Adult flies. Very small; orange-coloured, with black markings.

Eggs. Very small; slightly sausage-shaped.

Grubs. Orange or cream; less than $\frac{1}{4}$ in. long; differ from other fly maggots in that they are capable of reproducing themselves without first turning into flies. This means that the Cecid larvae may multiply rapidly in the beds without the grower becoming aware of their presence. It also means that insecticide dusts, which kill off the adult flies have no effect on the Cecid grub population in the beds. These have to be dealt with by means which are discussed under 'Fly Control'. Casing soil has been known to be infested with Cecid grubs.

Injury. The maggots feed on the spawn and at the roots of the mushrooms. They may burrow into the stems, or through the veil into the gills, where they are often found massed together in great numbers. Sometimes they swarm over the mushroom caps, which turn streaky, yellowed, and unmarketable.

(d) FLY CONTROL

It has been established by Dr. Thomas that fly larvae and eggs are not commonly found in the manure when it is first brought from the stables, and any eggs that are laid in the heap during the composting process will probably be destroyed either by the composting process itself or by the sweat-out. The danger period for infestation is during the days immediately after the sweat-out. Houses coming out of heat appear to hold an especial attraction for flies. These swarm in by the hundred from the surrounding countryside and lay their eggs in the cooling manure.

The flies themselves do little damage, beyond laying eggs and carrying disease spores and maggots about the house. It is the maggots that cause all the trouble. Unfortunately, since the maggots are deeply buried in the beds, only very drastic measures are effective against them, and the ruling principle in the war against the grubs must always be to keep down the fly population and so prevent the laying of eggs.

When it is considered that one female fly may produce several hundred eggs, each of which is capable of developing into an adult fly within three weeks and propogating many more, it will be readily appreciated that even a few flies can cause an infinite amount of trouble. It will also be seen that it is the first flies that it is important to catch. By the time the second generation of flies has taken hold, the situation is out of hand.

Means of exterminating the flies are discussed below, and a few desperate remedies for maggot infestations are given also.

DEALING WITH FLY INFESTATIONS

In pre-war days, the accepted method of tackling the fly menace was to treat the houses two or three times a week with a nicotine or pyrethrum dust. Since the war, however, pyrethrum and nicotine have largely been replaced by preparations containing D.D.T. (dichloro-diphenyl-trichloroethene) or B.H.C. (benzene hexachloride). These new preparations are so much superior in every way to the old-fashioned remedies that they may be said to have taken what was once one of the major problems of mushroom growing and turned it into a mere matter of routine hygiene.

Both D.D.T. and B.H.C. can be obtained either by themselves, or in combination with various other chemicals, and come in the form of sprays, dusts, 'fogs', and 'smoke bombs'. Indeed, the trouble nowadays is to keep up with the latest developments, for scarcely a month passes without some new concoction being brought on to the market and heralded as the most perfect insecticide treatment yet discovered.

Very often, these preparations have not been properly tested out and most of them are sold under proprietary names which give no hint as to the ingredients.

Fortunately for the grower, the M.G.A. publishes periodically a leaflet which gives the names of the newest insecticides and listed with each are the maker's name, the price, the methods of application, and an outline of the preparation's particular virtues. Furthermore, only those insecticides that have been tested out and found satisfactory are included. This pamphlet is a great help to the grower. It can be obtained from Yaxley for 2s. 6d., and is kept up to date and reprinted as necessary. No attempt will be made to give such a list here. Instead, a brief outline of the qualities of the various ingredients will be given.

(a) *Pyrethrum.* Swift-acting; paralyses flies instantly; effective for a few days only, so treatment has to be repeated about twice weekly; especially deadly to Sciarid flies; not toxic to humans, so can be used freely on the beds even during the cropping periods.

(b) *Nicotine.* Swift-acting; very effective against Phorid flies; potency extremely short-lived, so treatment may have to be given every second day; slightly toxic to humans, so it is inadvisable to use it on the beds while they are in flush.

(c) *D.D.T.* The most sensational of the new insecticides; deadly to flies; remarkably long-lived killing powers; a single dusting with D.D.T. has been known to keep a house free of flies for the duration of the crop. The question of its toxicity to humans has not yet been settled. Meantime, most growers play safe and give treatments only before cropping starts, or between flushes. If anti-fly treatment is urgently required while the mushrooms are on the beds, pyrethrum can be used instead. Many growers, in any case, continue to use pyrethrum as part of their insecticide routine, for one drawback to D.D.T. is that, though deadly, it is slow-acting. Flies that have been in contact with it may survive, apparently without ill-effect, for as long as twenty-four hours afterwards, during which period of grace, they may lay eggs. For bad infestations, it is a good plan to give a thorough dusting with pyrethrum for immediate immunity, and follow this with a D.D.T. treatment to make the cure more permanent.

A few growers have complained that the flies in *their* mushroom houses have developed an immunity to D.D.T. That flies can develop such an immunity has not yet been definitely established, but if it should prove to be the case, the problem can easily be solved by using B.H.C.

(*d*) *B.H.C.* Its qualities lie somewhere between those of D.D.T. and Pyrethrum. It is swifter acting, but less durable in effect than D.D.T.; slower acting and more lasting than Pyrethrum. Toxic to human beings, it should not be used when mushrooms are cropping. Even light treatments are liable to give the mushrooms an unpleasant taste.

These dusts used either in combination with each other or with other chemicals, form the basis of most of the insecticides on the market at the present time, and the control of fly infestations has now become a matter governed by individual experience and judgment.

Most insecticide routines adhere roughly to the following plan.

ROUTINE INSECTICIDE TREATMENT

The house is kept shut up as tightly as possible after the sweat-out, so as to hinder flies from gaining entry. Even after the beds have been spawned, very little ventilation is given, because Dr. Thomas has established that the growing mycelium does not require much oxygen.

When the beds have been cased, and ventilation becomes essential, active preventative measures must be taken, for although attempts have been made to prolong the period of 'fly exclusion' by ventilating only in the early morning and late evening when the flies are less active, and by fitting 30-mesh copper screens over the ventilators, neither of these courses has proved markedly successful. For one thing, the fine meshing in the screens is apt to become clogged with dirt and cut off ventilation completely. For another, the doors have to be opened during the day to admit workers and there is no way of stopping flies from entering at the same time.

Actually, most growers start giving insecticide treatments immediately the beds have been spawned, on the principle that if the beds are cool enough to spawn, they are cool enough to have eggs laid on them.

Generally, the first step is to dust or spray all the doors, ventilators, windows, and air-inlets with a strong D.D.T. preparation. This gives a permanent protection around every means of entry. Some growers even treat the outside of the house and the surrounding land with 'fog bombs', that fill the air with a fine D.D.T. dust. With these measures as a preliminary safeguard, there should be little chance of a fly infestation ever reaching serious proportions.

The house is now ready for its first insecticide treatment. This must be carried out with care, as it is important that a really strong concentration of dust is obtained, not only near the roof, but also at floor-level. Where the house is built with an upper gallery, dusting is usually carried out from the upper level first and then repeated at ground-level.

Before starting to dust, it is a good plan to spread the floor with a thick layer of nicotine-lime dust, so that insects that drop from the beds will not find refuge in cracks and crannies in out-of-the-way corners under the bottom shelves.

Dusting may be carried out either by hand bellows, or by using an electric duster. The operator should wear a mask. Apparatus for carrying out the dusting can usually be obtained from the firm supplying the dust.

Dusting should be repeated, either with the same or with an alternative insecticide, whenever the grower deems it advisable.

Preferably, treatments should be given immediately before the house is closed up for the night, as the dusts are most effective in a warm, still atmosphere.

Remedies such as kerosene light traps, and fumigation with sulphur and cyanide are now considered old-fashioned and are seldom used.

If a D.D.T. spray is used, make sure that it is not one of the many on the market that have a paraffin base, as these sprays, used in a mushroom house, would cause rose-comb.

FLY LARVAE IN THE BEDS

The simplest way of getting rid of the larvae in the beds is to keep the house warm (70° F. to 75° F.). This speeds up the rate of development of the maggots, so that in the shortest possible time, they turn into flies and come out to be killed. During the period of development, unfortunately, the maggots must be left to do their worst.

Where Cecid fly larvae have invaded the beds, more direct action is needed, since these may multiply rapidly without becoming flies.

One method of tackling them is to dry out the beds slightly and then give a light watering. This attracts the maggots to the surface, where they can be dealt with by:

(1) Dusting the surface of the beds with a pyrethrum-nicotine dust.

(2) Fumigating the house with hydrogen-cyanide gas. This is a dangerous and complicated process and is not recommended. It is in any case not so effective as the simpler dust treatment.

Cecid flies have been known to come in with the casing soil, but the steam sterilizing or chloropicrin treatment described in Chapter Eight should eliminate all danger of contamination from this source.

Experiments have been carried out in Denmark and in this country to test the effect of mixing D.D.T. and other insecticides through the compost. The scientists in the Research laboratories have not so far reached any very definite conclusion, but growers who have tried it say that when mixed into the manure before composting, the D.D.T. appears to have lost all its potency by the time the manure is composted, and when mixed in during filling, it has an adverse effect on the crop.

These are purely unscientific findings, however, and the research laboratories may be able to give valuable guidance on this subject when their experiments have had time to bear fruit.

[2] Insect Pests

(a) MITES

There are several varieties of mites, all very small, so that usually a hand lens is required to detect their presence.

(i) TYROGLYPHUS SP. (MUSHROOM MITE)

Adult. About half the size of a pin head; white or yellow, with long bristles on its body; eight legs; moves slowly.

Eggs. Unexpectedly large, considering the size of the mite. They hatch in eight to fourteen days.

Larvae. Tiny; six legs; in ten days, they shed their skins and become 'nymphs' with eight legs. After two more feeding periods and moults, the nymphs become adults.

Injury. The mites, grubs, and nymphs, feed on the spawn, damaging it and sometimes killing it altogether. They also eat holes in the mushroom caps and pin-heads.

(ii) RHIZOGLYPHUS PHYLLOXERA (BULB MITE)

These mites are similar in appearance to the Tyroglyphidae, but are fatter and have shorter bristles. They feed mainly on the spawn pieces and on the spawn mycelium. Between two of the moults, the nymphs become 'hypopi'. This is a dormant stage, during which they cease to feed. Instead, they attach themselves by means of suckers to the bodies of flies or insects, or to the clothing of workers and so get themselves carried to new feeding-grounds in hitherto uninfested beds.

(iii) LINOPODES ANTENNAEPES (THE LONG-LEGGED MITE)

Adults. Light yellow or reddish brown; larger than other species; easily recognized by their distinctive front legs, which are twice as long as their bodies and in constant motion.

These mites are difficult to control, as they can move very quickly, but they are susceptible to nicotine and temperatures as low as 100° F. will kill them.

Usually, they gather at the base of a mushroom stalk and cut off the feeder roots. The stalk becomes 'waisted' and slightly reddish.

(iv) HISTIOSTOMA GRACILIPES

Adults. Very small, with angular lumpy bodies, blunt at the end; they develop hypopi, which are reddish brown in colour.

These mites feed on the spawn, on dead and decaying mushrooms, and on the roots of healthy mushrooms.

(v) TARSONEMUS FLORICOLUS

Adults. Creamy or brown; oval; shiny; very small; six legs when hatched, but eventually they develop eight.

They turn the base of the mushroom stalk brown, and swarm like a brown dust over the surface of the pin-heads and mushroom caps. Eventually the pin-heads die.

All affected mushrooms should be picked off without delay and destroyed.

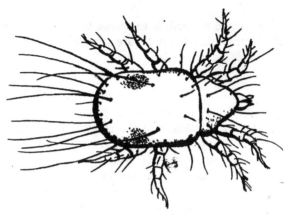

FIG. 16. THE TYRO MITE

(vi) PIGMAEOPHORUS AMERICANUS (PIGMY MITE)

Adults. Reddish in colour; very small; angular, with blunt ends. They may appear unexpectedly in enormous numbers and disappear as rapidly. Usually, they do not cause much damage, but they swarm over the surface of the mushroom caps, till the mushrooms look as though they had been sprinkled with red pepper.

Dr. Thomas, experimenting with a 0·25 per cent thiocyanate solution, has obtained fairly good results against this mite. Another,

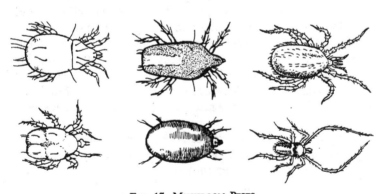

FIG. 17. MUSHROOM PESTS

Left to right
Top: Rhizo Mite: Pigmy Mite: Gamasid Mite
Bottom: Histo Mite: Tarso Mite: Long-Legged Mite

45

but more troublesome method, is to spread the surface of the bed with a sheet of wet muslin. The mites are attracted on to the muslin, which is then rolled up and boiled.

MITE CONTROL

Mites normally live in the soil. Usually, they gain entry to the mushroom house by crawling into the manure while it is in the composting yard, or they may be present in unsterilized casing soil. Bad infestations are sometimes got in houses that have not been adequately decontaminated after the previous crop.

Prevention is important, as there is as yet no very satisfactory method of dealing with mites. Composting yards should, if possible, have a concrete base, and should be thoroughly cleaned and disinfected before a new load of manure is laid down. Houses should be cleaned, sprayed, and either steam-heated or fumigated before being refilled. Bed-boards need scrubbing, disinfecting, and a period of drying out, preferably in the open air and in sunlight. Steam-heating the house before the spent manure is carted out prevents contamination being spread around the plant by the old manure. A good peak heat assisted by live steam or fumigation, and a thick layer of nicotine dust on the floor of the house should take care of any mites that are present in the newly filled beds. A layer of 1 lb. 3 per cent nicotine dust per 40 sq. ft. on the floor whenever a dusting for fly control is given not only makes the fly treatment more effective, but also helps to check any mite infestations that might be starting.

Houses that have become infested with mites should be dried out for a while, if possible, and the bed-boards should be extra thoroughly disinfected. Use sterilized casing soil for the next crop, and see that the composting yard is adequately decontaminated before fresh manure is laid down on it. Ensure a good peak heat at the next sweat-out.

For treating composting yards, several new miticides, such as hexaethyl tetraphosphate, are gaining favour, but the grower is best to make his choice from an up-to-date catalogue.

FOR BAD MITE INFESTATIONS

Preferably, treatment should be given between flushes, and all mushrooms should be picked from the beds before starting.

PLATE 19

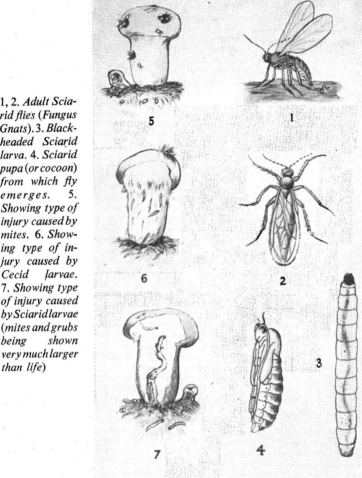

1, 2. *Adult Sciarid flies (Fungus Gnats).* 3. *Blackheaded Sciarid larva.* 4. *Sciarid pupa (or cocoon) from which fly emerges.* 5. *Showing type of injury caused by mites.* 6. *Showing type of injury caused by Cecid larvae.* 7. *Showing type of injury caused by Sciarid larvae (mites and grubs being shown very much larger than life)*

PLATE 20

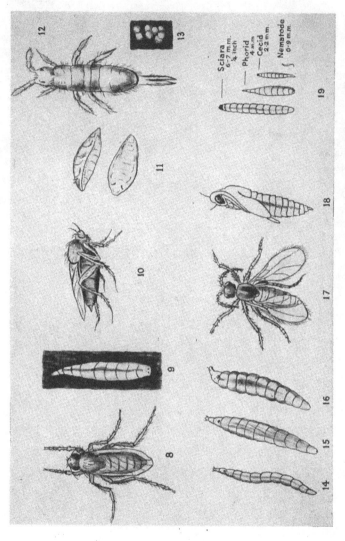

8. *Adult Phorid fly* (see also 10). 9. *Phorid larva.* 10. *Adult Phorid fly* (see also 8). 11. *Two views of Phorid pupa.* 12. *A silvery springtail.* 13. *Springtail eggs, many times enlarged.* 14, 15, 16. *Various sizes of Cecid larvae.* 17. *Cecid fly.* 18. *Cecid pupa.* 19. *Comparative sizes of various grubs*

First dry out the beds slightly, and then give a light watering. This attracts the mites to the surface of the beds. The beds should now be either sprayed with a solution of 1 oz. nicotine sulphate per gal. of water, or dusted with a 6 per cent nicotine-clay dust, allowing 1 lb. per 90 sq. ft. of bed space. When applying the dust, workers must wear masks.

Since these treatments only deal with the mites on the surface of the manure, they must be repeated every two days till the infestation is controlled. Fortunately, the drying-out delays the next flush, and it can be retarded still further by using the nicotine spray for the first treatment and dust for all subsequent treatments, except for a final spraying, just before the beds are watered back into production.

GAMASID MITE (RED SPIDER)

These spiders are welcome guests in a mushroom house, as, instead of damaging the crop, they feed on the other mites. They are reddish in colour, move rapidly, and are about the same size as the *Linopodes antennaepes*, but have not got such long front legs.

(*b*) SPRINGTAILS

These small insects live in the soil and crawl into the manure whenever they get an opportunity. There are several species, all very similar to each other.

    (i) *Lepidocyrtus lanuginosus* (the red springtail).
    (ii) *Achorutes armatum* (the grey springtail).
    (iii) *Lepidocyrtus cyaneus* (the silver springtail).
    (iv) *Proisotoma* (the spawn springtail—light grey).

All varieties are very active, move rapidly, and can spring a distance of several inches by means of a little lever in their tails. Occasionally, they are found in heaps on the floors of the mushroom houses, but most often, they collect in colonies round the newly planted spawn pieces. At best, they merely chew up the spawn piece and impair the spawn run, but they have been known to devour the spawn piece completely and stop the spawn run altogether. Their presence can be detected by lifting the spawn piece out and placing it on a sheet of paper under a bright light. The springtails are attracted by the light and crawl out to investigate.

Besides eating the spawn, the springtails lay innumerable tiny round-shaped eggs in the manure, and later, during cropping, they may eat holes in the mushrooms.

Control. Treatment is the same as for mite infestations. Some growers spray the bottom beds with a nicotine solution as part of the 'pest control' routine, whether there are signs of pests or not. This is very effective, because the bottom beds are usually the first to become infected and if the pests are controlled here, they are not likely to reach the upper beds at all.

Heavy infestations. Heavy infestations are usually due either to a poor sweat-out or to infected casing soil and should never occur. Treatment is the same as for mite infestations. Nicotine is extremely effective against springtails. D.D.T. has been tried, but does not seem to do much good. A troublesome, but fairly satisfactory method devised by Dr. Thomas is to spread muslin sheets over the beds, scatter paradichlorobenzene crystals on top, and cover the whole with sheets of paper to keep the gas confined. The beds are left covered for five to six hours.

Any heaps of springtails found on the floors should be swept up and burnt. Nicotine dust scattered in the doorways will prevent the insects crawling in from outside.

(c) NEMATODES (EELWORMS)

These small worms have recently made 'Mushroom News'. For years, growers have been puzzled by a mysterious disease that kills the spawn, turns the manure dank and foul, and covers the surface of the beds with a thin grey mould. Research in America has revealed that the trouble is caused by eelworms, and a most interesting and instructive pamphlet on the subject has been written by Dr. Thomas and Dr. Mitchell of Pennsylvania State College Agriculture Experimental Station. This leaflet describes in detail all that has so far been discovered about the problem and the work of the various scientists who have been concerned with the research, and it is well worth studying. Only a brief résumé will be given here.

Appearance. Very small worms that can be seen only with the help of a hand lens or microscope; they are thin, wriggly, thread-like, and scarcely a millimetre in length; white, but transparent like glass; smooth-skinned—i.e. not jointed or segmented; no legs; they move by swimming like an eel through the moisture in the soil and manure. They may give birth to living young or lay eggs.

Eggs. Minute; oval; white; transparent; hatch in twenty-four hours.

Young. Exceedingly small; transparent; very active; shed their skins several times during the period of growth to maturity, which may take several days.

To test for the presence of nematodes, wrap a piece of suspect compost in a muslin bag and suspend it in water overnight. Samples of the water examined through a microscope in the morning will reveal eelworms, if any were present in the muslin bag to begin with.

Two main types of nematode have been discovered.

(*a*) *Ditylenchus spp.* These are known as the 'Stylet' type. The mouth of each worm has a small, needle-like probe, shaped like a spear, which it inserts right into the 'pipe-lines' of mushroom mycelium and so sucks the food direct from the mycelium threads. The spawn dies, and so do the mushrooms on the surface of the beds. The manure rots, turns black, and becomes wet and foul-smelling. The mould which appears on the top of the casing soil is not a part of the disease, but is a parasitic fungus that feeds on the nematodes. The mould itself is quite distinctive, being very fine and velvety and light in colour.

(*b*) *Rhabditis spp.* Instead of a needle-like, probing mouth, these worms have hollow, tube-like mouths and throats, into which they suck food and bacteria. They are not so much associated with the blackness and rotting of the manure, as with a 'redness' of the manure. Apart from this redness, the manure and spawn appear to be perfectly normal, but no mushrooms grow. These worms are also suspected of carrying the bacteria that cause 'Bacterial Pit'.

Injury. Wholesale destruction of the spawn mycelium causing reduction or loss of crop. The spreading of bacteria. The first hint of the presence of the nematodes is usually either (i) the appearance of the parasitic mould, or (ii) large unproductive areas on the beds, or (iii) the 'caving-in' of the casing soil due to the rotting away of the manure below. Normally, the trouble does not show itself until the later flushes.

Source. Nematodes were found in almost every soil sample that was examined by Dr. Thomas and Dr. Mitchell, who then concluded that they are normally present in all soils, but that they thrive best in moist, warm, undisturbed earth, such as meadow lands. Cultivated land is not usually so thickly infested. It is not thought that nematodes are present in the manure when it is first brought to the plant, but it is believed that they crawl into it from infested composting yards, bed-boards, and casing soil.

Prevention. First guard against infection from the composting yard, or from the lorries that carry the manure to the plant. Most of the disinfectants hitherto employed in mushroom growing have proved ineffective against nematodes, and so far, the only satisfactory method of dealing with them is to 'steam heat' whatever is contaminated. A temperature of 140°F. for one to three days gives a good kill. A concrete composting yard is less likely to carry infection than one with an earth surface.

Any eelworms present in the manure should be destroyed during the composting process if it is perfectly carried out, so that every portion of the compost lies for a time in the hottest part of the heap. Unfortunately, this does not always happen. Careless turning, or badly designed manure-turners may produce heaps containing large patches of compost that have never been in the centre of the pile at all.

A good sweat-out should complete the destruction of the pests in the manure, but this is unlikely to be achieved without the aid of live steam. Fumigation with cyanide or sulphur is no use whatsoever against nematodes.

Disinfectants having proved useless for cleaning infested houses and bed-boards, prolonged drying out of the premises has been tried, but both the nematodes and their eggs appear to be able to go into a kind of dehydrated state, in which apparently lifeless condition they seem capable of surviving indefinitely, for, as soon as moisture becomes plentiful, the eggs hatch and the worms become active as before. Steam heating the empty houses and bed-boards is the only effective remedy so far discovered, and it is more deadly if the houses and bed-boards are sprayed beforehand to make the worms more active. The eggs can survive at higher temperatures than the worms.

Casing soil that contains nematodes should never be sterilized with formaldehyde. The formaldehyde has no effect on the nematodes, but it destroys the parasitic mould that feeds on them. Without the mould to keep them in check, a nematode infestation may reach deadly proportions. Sterilization with chloropicrin is fairly satisfactory, but it is difficult to get a strong enough concentration of gas for a long enough period to give a complete 'clean-up'. Usually, a good many nematodes survive, especially if the soil is moist and the gas cannot penetrate freely. Steam sterilizing is again recommended, and the soil must be well happed afterwards, to keep the heat in it for as long as possible. If the outsides of the heap cool down before the rest, nematodes from there may reinfect the whole pile.

Another way in which the pile may be reinfected is by contact with the soil storage floor. Concrete floors are easier to keep clean than soil floors, but some growers store their soil on sheets of corrugated iron raised on blocks above floor-level. Reinfestation is not likely if the soil is dry, as the nematodes cannot travel without water to swim in.

Control. Since the eelworms are deep in the compost there is no effective method of dealing with them, once the beds are spawned. All that can be done is to try to prevent the nematodes from spreading by drying out infected beds completely.

SOWBUGS (WOOD LICE, PILLBUGS)

Grey, oval crustaceans, about half an inch long, with fourteen legs. They roll into a ball if disturbed and hide in the dark under boards and in crevices.

Only heavy infestations do much damage and these are fortunately rare. Usually the sowbugs come in along with the manure and are killed during the peak heat. Any that survive will eat the spawn and the mushrooms. They can be picked off by hand or trapped with baits poisoned with paris green, but such baits must only be placed where there is no danger of their coming in contact with the mushrooms. D.D.T. and Pyrethrum are especially effective against sowbugs, and the normal routine insect and fly control programme keeps them well in hand.

SLUGS, SNAILS

These are sometimes found in damp houses. They eat holes in the mushrooms and should be picked off by hand and destroyed.

MILLIPEDES

These may occur in ground beds. Control by soaking the ground with 1 gal. cresylic acid per 25 gals. water. The ground must be well aired after treatment before new beds are laid down as cresylic acid causes 'deformed' mushrooms.

WIREWORMS

About an inch long, reddish brown, six legs, thin, hard-skinned. Do little damage.

LOOPER CATERPILLARS

Brown or green, spotted, grow to about an inch long. Eat holes in the mushroom caps. Seldom appear in sufficient numbers to do much damage. They can be picked off by hand or treated with insecticide dusts.

BEETLES

These do little damage, beyond carrying disease spores about. Pick off by hand or treat with D.D.T. and fly dusts.

RATS AND MICE

They eat holes in the mushrooms and tear the beds to pieces to get at the straw and grain spawn. Use traps or poisoned bait, but poison injurious to humans must not be used on or near the mushroom beds.

INSECTS AND MITES

THESE are the worst enemies the grower has to fight. It is apparently hard for the grower to realize the danger from a few insects while the spawn is running, for he knows that every house, good or bad, will be full of insects in the later stages without noticeable harm. Therefore, we can not emphasize too much the fact that one insect at spawning may do more harm than a thousand after the spawn is run.

It is not possible to give detailed descriptions here of the various insects and mites*. The Sciarid flies, or mushroom gnats, are small black flies whose larvae are white maggots one-eighth inch long, with black heads. The larvae attack the spawn and mushrooms. They will be commonest in the wetter spots of the bed of spawn, and the bed will turn reddish brown with the disappearance of the spawn. In the mushroom they cause black streaks in the stem and worm holes in the caps. They are the chief cause of small mushrooms dying on the bed. The adult flies carry mites, molds and diseases, and are often responsible for outbreaks of flour mold.

The Phorid flies, called "manure flies" by the growers, are about the same size as the Sciarids, but shorter in body. They have a color which is black, but with less sheen than the other fly, and more smoky in appearance, sometimes being only gray. They usually abound around the ends of the compost heap. They will go from here into the houses and lay eggs in the beds, and this is the common method of infesting the houses. The larva is about the size of the Sciarid larva but does not have the black head. The larvae attack the compost as well as the spawn, and only attack the mushrooms infrequently. On the whole, they are less harmful than the other kinds of flies, but seem to be harder to kill. The adults are very active, and spread rapidly.

---

* THOMAS, C. A., Bulletin No. 270, Penna. State College Expt. Station 1931.

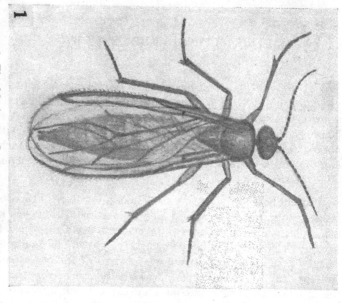

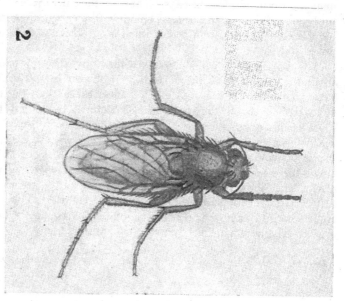

1. The Mushroom Gnat or Sciarid Fly, *Sciara coprophila* Lintner. 2. The Manure Fly or Phorid Fly, *Aphiochaeta agarici* Lintner. Much enlarged. Drawings by C. A. Thomas.

The Mushroom Springtail,
Achorutes armatus Nic.
Much enlarged. Drawing
by C. A. Thomas.

The springtails are tiny gray or white cigar shaped insects. They attack the spawn, causing the most harm when they are common within the first week or two. In the later stages of the crop they may be found all over the mushrooms, beds, and floor.

Mites resemble small spiders, almost colorless and transparent; it usually requires careful examination of the beds to detect them, unless they are moving. Several species attack in different ways, but in general they attack the spawn, or puncture and suck the sap from the heavy feeding strands at the base of the mushroom. The mushrooms on infested beds are reddish about the base of the stems, and stand high above the soil on a single central root.

It must be remembered that the insects do the most harm in the beds, where there is no way to kill them. Not even all the adult insects come out of the bed where they can be killed. Prevention is the only control. All the traps, sprays, fumigants, poisons, and dusts must be considered only as helps to keep the infestations as low as possible, and to prevent their spread to other houses.

The insects come to the house from spent manure if not hauled away. They burrow into the soil inside and about the house. Some of them breed in the cooler parts of the compost pile and wet spots on the ground nearby. Some are present in the manure when it arrives. There seems now to be only one reasonably certain means of eliminating them, and that is by heating the house to above 130°F. in every part of the beds, after the compost has been put in. It is fortunate that this rise in temperature is beneficial in other ways and does no harm. The grower should let nothing interfere with this heating.

In most houses, air leaks prevent the air temperature rising as high as the beds. This combination will draw the insects out of the beds, where the majority of them may be killed by fumigation if the air temperature alone does not kill them.

Two methods of fumigation for this purpose are in use. The safest for the crop is probably the cyanide fumigation. This was formerly carried out by scattering on the damp aisle of the house one pound of Calcium cyanide for each 1000 cubic feet of air

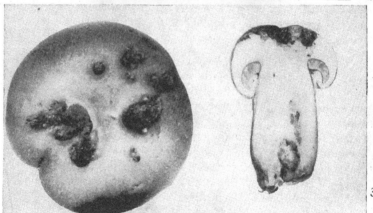

(1) The Mushroom Mite, *Tyroglyphus lintneri* Osborn; (2) mushroom injured by mites around base of stem and standing on central root only; (3) mushrooms eaten by mites. Drawing much enlarged. Drawing and lower photograph by C. A. Thomas.

space in the building according to directions with the package. However, ordinary cyanides are not recommended on account of the danger to human life. The odor of cyanide gas is not sufficient to give warning and in many places its use is now prohibited. A new material which avoids this danger is now the subject of experiment and may soon replace ordinary cyanide for the purpose. This is a mixture of cyanide and chlorine which evolves hydrocyanic acid and a warning gas, cyanogen chloride. It appears that $1\frac{1}{4}$ pounds of this material per 1000 cubic feet is sufficient to give a good kill of insects. In cities where ordinary cyanides are prohibited by law this material containing the warning gas may be used. It may be used safely in any mushroom house and may be left in for 12 hours for the best effect, and will disappear from the house in a few minutes after opening. The house should be sealed up as tightly as possible and the beds should be above 130°F.

The second method is fumigation with sulphur. One pound of sulphur per 1000 cubic feet is burned in pans. This treatment is as effective against insects and mites, but often results in a general infection of the bed surfaces with molds. Although these molds are not known to be harmful to the crop, the acidity of compost to which their growth is due is not felt to be the best thing for the spawn when it reaches this layer. Sulphur fumigation is therefore recommended only under the following conditions: the beds must have heated long enough to dry off well on the surface; the house must be ready to open and must be cooled and aired out within four hours after the treatment. With sulphur it is imperative that the grower wait until ready to cool, because the necessary opening is bound to cool off the beds.

One of the difficulties of insect control is the comparative slowness of the lowest beds to heat up. This may be overcome by circulating the air as the temperature rises, using two to four fans turned upward or downward in the center aisle.

Every grower should lay a sheet of fly paper on each bed after it is spawned and watch the collection of springtails and mites. Fly paper placed under a small window in the house will in the same way make visible the degree of infestation by flies. This is far more reliable than direct observation.

After mushrooms appear, insects are sure to become common. If houses are then filled nearby, they will be infested at once except in the coldest weather. *Growers are therefore urged to com-*

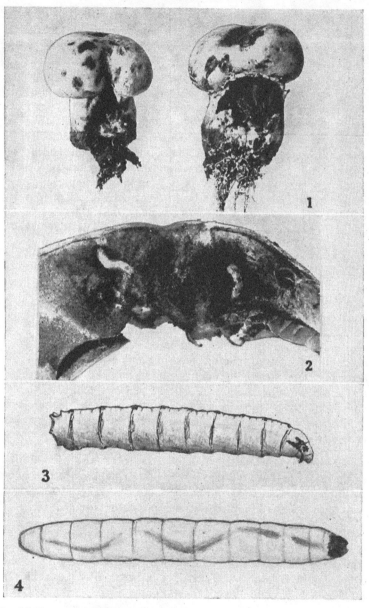

1. Mushrooms injured by Sciarid Fly Larvae, followed by secondary infection of Spot organism. 2. Section through mushroom cap, enlarged, showing Sciarid Larvae. 3. Larva of Phorid Fly. Much enlarged. 4. Larva of Sciarid Fly. Much enlarged. Photographs by C. A. Thomas.

plete the filling of the whole plant in a short time, and it is suggested that the spawning of all houses should be completed before the crop begins in the first house. All houses less than 500 feet apart should be considered as one plant. Likewise, all houses should be cleaned out, fumigated as already described, and the spent manure removed from the 500 ft. area, before any of the houses are filled again. Aside from proper composting and heating, the filling of the whole plant as a unit is probably the most important principle of mushroom management.

Several useful control measures for certain insects are described in Appendix E. These are more or less effective insofar as the exposed insects are usually killed, but in nearly all cases have to be repeated frequently as more insects emerge from the beds. Generally speaking, the development of insects can be retarded by lowering the temperature of the house to 48° or 50° F. (This would not be done until after the spawn has run full.) There is often a question whether this does not retard the crop as much as the insects, with no gain to the grower. The lowering of the temperature would probably pay in the case of flies, but not in the case of mites.

Mice are often a serious pest in mushroom houses. They come into the warm houses during cold weather, and make holes in the surface of the compost to obtain pieces of grain or other food in the beds. In some cases they are attracted by the odor of the spawn and tear out the pieces. After the beds are cased they literally plow the soil in search of garlic and other bulbs and seeds. If only a few mice are in the house they may usually be caught in traps or killed with poison. In worse cases fumigation with cyanide as described on page 60 may be resorted to.

MUSHROOM INSECTS; THEIR BIOLOGY AND CONTROL.

by C. A. Thomas

Reprinted from Bulletin 270, The Pennsylvania State College School of Agriculture and Experiment Station, October, 1931.

A considerable number of mites and insects have been recorded as injurious to mushrooms and mycelium, but only the following have thus far been found to be of much economic importance in Pennsylvania:

MAJOR PESTS.

Common Name	Scientific Name	Order or Family
Mushroom mite	*Tyroglyphus lintneri* Osborn	Acarina
Long-legged mite	*Linopodes antennaepes* Banks	Acarina
Mushroom springtail	*Achorutes armatus* Nic	Collembola
Silvery springtail	*Lepidocyrtus cyaneus* Tullb	Collembola
Fungus gnat	*Neosciara pauciseta* Felt	Mycetophilidae
Fungus gnat	*Sciara coprophila* Lintner	Mycetophilidae
Fungus gnat	*Sciara multiseta* Felt	Mycetophilidae
Fungus gnat	*Sciara agraria* Felt	Mycetophilidae
Manure fly	*Aphiochaeta albidihalteris* Felt	Phoridae
Manure fly	*Aphiochaeta agarici* Lintner	Phoridae

MINOR PESTS.

Eelworms, *Nematodes* (Roundworms) may occasionally be injurious.

Sowbugs (Woodlice), *Porcellio laevis* Koch. and related species, *Crustacea.*

"Looper" caterpillar, *Metalectra quadrisignata* Wkr., *Noctuidae.* Gall gnats, undetermined species of *Cecidomyiidae.*

Not all of these are injurious in any mushroom house at one time; they are the species which have caused injury at various places. Under favorable conditions, any one of them may become abundant enough to cause serious damage.

The so-called "red-spiders" found in mushroom houses usually cause no injury to the crop but may be of considerable value by feeding on Mushroom mites and springtails. These "spiders" are mites belonging to the family *Gamasidae* (Parasitidae). They vary from flesh-color to brick red, have waving front legs (not nearly so long as those of the *Linopodes* mite), and can run quite rapidly.

KEY TO INJURIES CAUSED BY MUSHROOM PESTS.

Frequently the grower finds his spawn eaten, or holes in his mushrooms, but may not find any insects at the time. Therefore he is at a loss as to the identity of the pest. In order to assist growers in diagnosis, the following table is presented:

I. Injury to spawn piece or to the mycelium in the bed.

    A. Spawn or mycelium destroyed:

        1. Spawn pieces do not grow out into the manure.

            a. Is infested with small white headless worms—PHORID FLY larvae.

            b. No worms found in the spawn piece or mycelium, but the mycelium does not grow into the manure. Manure may be too wet, too acid, or perhaps not properly composted.

        2. Mycelium is destroyed in the manure, and the manure may be broken down into a damp mass of chewed material:

            a. By black-headed white worms up to one-fourth inch long—SCIARA FLY larvae.

            b. By very small, grayish or silvery jumping insects. These also are frequently seen in gray piles in the aisles—SPRINGTAILS.

II. Injury to caps and stems of the mushrooms.

    A. Holes in the surface or inside the mushroom tissue:

        1. Galleries or tunnels within the mushroom tissue, sometimes reaching the surface. These may extend from the base of the stem up into the gills and cap. The latter is sometimes entirely spongy and dark inside. Stem may crack open and turn dark. Small mushrooms are frequently spongy, yellow and stop growing:

            a. Contain white larvae with black head capsule—SCIARA FLY larvae.

b. Contain white larvae without black head capsule
—PHORID FLY larvae.

2. Irregular holes eaten into the surface of stem or cap. Small mushrooms hollowed out inside. These holes may penetrate into the cap some distance and contain small, dark slimy pits in which are very minute bristly white creatures resembling small drops of glycerin—TYROGLYPHID MITES.

3. Small irregular holes eaten into the stem or cap, which may sometimes be honeycombed. May contain tiny gray jumping insects, which are also found piled in the aisles, crawling up the posts or grouped on the caps after watering the beds—MUSHROOM SPRINGTAILS.

4. Larger holes chewed into the surface of cap or stem. These holes are not full of tiny dirty pits, and the tissue remains white or nearly so. May be caused WOODLICE, LOOPER CATERPILLARS, MICE or RATS.

5. Base of stem rusty-colored, very much constricted and with very few roots holding it to the bed. Has been chewed. Small very active, longlegged mites running on the mushrooms and beds. Flesh-colored to nearly white, have a lighter T-shaped mark on the back and very long front legs, which are continually waving—LONG-LEGGED MITE (*Linopodes antennaepes* Banks), May also be caused by *naepes* Banks). May also be caused by other mites.

6. Small mushrooms covered with tiny reddish powder-like creatures, which may become abundant enough to prevent their growth—HYPOPI of TYROGLYPHID MITE or a stage of the LINOPODES MITE.

7. Caps turn brown and watery and break down. Myriads of very small, thread-like, whitish worms with undulating or waving movements. NEMATODES (Eelworms).

B. Mushrooms deformed or split. Gills and "warts" may appear on the top of the caps, which may have good tissue within, however. This condition can be caused by kerosene or other oils used as sprays, although doubtless there are other causes. . . .

MUSHROOM FLIES.

It is probable that mushroom flies are the most wide-spread and most generally destructive insect enemies of the cultivated mushroom. The actual injury is not caused by the flies but by their young or larvae, which feed in the manure, on the mycelium or inside the stem or cap of the growing mushroom.

For convenience of description these flies are grouped as *Sciarids* or Fungus gnats, and *Phorids* or manure flies. These will be referred to throughout this paper as *Sciarids* and *Phorids* respectively.

SCIARIDS OR FUNGUS GNATS.

At least three species of the dipterous family *Mycetophilidae*, or fungus gnats, inhabit mushroom houses. Of these the most abundant and injurious in Pennsylvania are *Sciara coprophila* Lintner, *S. multiseta* Felt and *Neosciara pauciseta* Felt. Since these are all similar in appearance they will be treated here as one species although there are some minor differences in their biology and life history.

Description, Biology, and Injury. These flies are fairly slender, with comparatively long legs and wings. They are black or dark brown, and have slender, thread-like antennae or "feelers." The figures on Plate 2 show the various stages of these flies.

Sciarid flies normally inhabit wild mushrooms, manure piles, and greenhouses, but the conditions found in mushroom houses are very favorable for their development. Most of them enter the houses as larvae in the manure, but many adults also enter through the doors and ventilators. Once within the house the fly lays its eggs upon the manure.

After casing, when the manure is covered and the mushrooms are growing, the eggs are deposited on the casing soil, at the base of the mushroom stem, and on the stem, gills or cap. The eggs hatch in 4 to 6 days at mushroom house temperatures. There is much variation in the time required for the eggs and other stages to develop.

The larvae or "worms" which hatch from the eggs are white, shiny, nearly transparent, and have a small black chitinous head. The contents of the food canal are plainly visible through the body wall. If these larvae hatch within the beds they feed upon the mycelium or spawn, chewing it into tiny bits and finally destroying it entirely if unchecked. . . . Sometimes the tiny mushrooms called "pinheads", just breaking through the soil, are attacked by several larvae at once and completely hollowed out. They then turn yellowish-brown and fail to develop any further. Occasionally a whole crop may be lost in this manner.

The larva is full grown when it reaches the length of about seven millimeters (approximately one-fourth inch). The larval stage lasts from 10 to 14 days, depending on the temperature, moisture, etc. Evidently it molts or sheds its skin several times during its development. Sometimes the larvae will appear on the casing soil in immense numbers, crawling in all directions. Apparently, there is a moisture relation connected with it, for this usually occurs after watering the beds.

When the larva has attained its full size of one-fourth inch, it stops feeding, crawls down to the soil or manure, spins a very thin silken cocoon and then sheds its skin. It thus becomes the pupa, the stage in which the organs and tissues of the larva are transformed into those of the adult fly. The pupa stage, lasts about 4 to 7 days. During this period no feeding occurs. Near the end of the pupal period the pupa pushes itself up through the top of the cocoon and to the vicinity of the soil or manure surface. Sometimes the pupa is formed within the mushroom, but much more frequently in the soil. Those larvae which crawl upon the casing soil may even go through the pupa stage there without spinning a cocoon. . . .

The flies are positively phototropic, that is, they are attracted to daylight, and to artificial lights within the house. . . .

There is some indication that when several varieties of mushrooms are growing in a house, the fly larvae attack chiefly the brown and cream varieties in preference to white varieties. This has not been thoroughly investigated. . . .

Control. Many methods have been recommended for the control of mushroom flies, but only a few give even a fair degree of control. Prevention should always be the first objective. The manure should be thoroughly composted, and all beds, including the bottom beds, should come to a temperature of at least 130°F. Raising the bottom beds and the use of the fans should be practiced at this time. Screening the ventilators and doors may also have value. Fumigation, dusting, or other measures should begin as soon as the manure reaches its top heat and should be repeated at intervals throughout the season as needed. Too many growers wait until they are over-run with flies before attempting to control them. When we remember how many eggs a female fly can lay, and that there is a new generation of flies about every three weeks, the importance of killing the first flies that appear is evident.

The following methods are used in mushroom houses:

Light Traps. These make use of the positive phototropism or natural attraction of the flies to artificial and natural light. Several forms of traps have been devised, of which the following are the most effective:

Electric light-kerosene trap. A flat pan is suspended a few inches below an electric light placed on the ceiling, above the ends of the middle aisle. A small amount of kerosene is placed in this pan. The heat from the light slowly volatilizes the kerosene, thus adding to the effectiveness of the trap. The pan should be at least 15 inches square. Large numbers of mushroom flies have been caught in these traps, a high percentage of them being females containing eggs. However, these traps do not catch all of the flies, nor do they always catch the females before they have deposited their eggs; but if they are put into operation immediately after the heating of the manure and are continued throughout the season they will catch the excess of flies. Traps should be supplemented with dusting or fumigation. Instead of kerosene pans, many growers hang sticky fly papers near the lights. The use of the light-kerosene trap was developed in France at least 40 years ago.

Windows. Single panes of glass, placed in the doors or in the end walls of the house, let in daylight which is attractive to flies. These panes should be placed about half way up in the door in the sunny end of the house. To catch the attracted flies sticky fly paper may be tacked at the bottom and side of the glass. The sticky material also can be painted on wrapping paper tacked in the same position. Some growers paint it lightly on cheese cloth and tack this directly across the glass so that the light shines through it. Whichever method is used, these sticky traps should be frequently renewed, as they are quickly covered with flies and will not catch more. . . .

Pyrethrum and Other Dusts. A number of commercial dusts have been used by mushroom growers. The active ingredient of most of these dusts is pyrethrum. Formerly, a practically pure pyrethrum powder was used exclusively against mushroom flies, but since its rise in price, dusts containing pyrethrum combined with other constituents have been developed. These other constituents are mainly inert materials which act as carriers for the pyrethrum. One of the dusts now in common use combines 60 per cent pyrethrum with 40 per cent of an inert light earth. Another combines pyrethrum and tobacco dust. Another more recent dust is composed of pyrethrum plus a stomach poison. These combination dusts are considerably cheaper than the pure pyrethrum, and generally remain suspended in the air for a longer period. At the same time, they are quite toxic to the flies. The cheapest dust is not always the best; toxicity or kill of the flies is the principal factor to be sought.

As with fumigants, the use of dusts should begin as soon as the manure has lost its high temperature, and should be repeated at intervals of a few days, as necessary. At low temperatures the dusts and the flies are both less active, and the flies will stay under the beds and back of the boards where the dust cannot get at them. Therefore, the house should be at least 60°F. for several hours before dusting. It should remain at this higher temperature during the dusting and for several hours afterward, as some of the dusts will float in the air and be effective for some time. The house may be dusted in the evening and remain closed until the next morning.

From 2 to 3 pounds of the dust should be used each time in a single 60-foot house. This is at the rate of about 2½ to 3 ounces of dust per 100 cubic feet of air space. The dusting should be done throughly, upstairs and down, and in all of the aisles, and an attempt should be made to get it up under the beds where many flies rest. Dust thoroughly near the doors, where flies are common. A duster with crank and fan blower is the best type to use. Small dust masks may be used to protect the nose and throat of the operator.

Although there have been a few complaints of injury, supposedly caused by several of the pyrethrum combination dusts, investigation generally shows it to have been caused by other factors. Heavy dusting when the mushroom caps are wet may leave a yellowish stain on the caps, especially on white mushrooms, but dry caps usually show little of the stain.

Recently an ingenious method was observed in which the grower dusted directly over a horizontal electric fan placed in the central aisle. The air currents distributed the dust quite thoroughly with a minimum of labor. The fan was moved wherever needed along the aisle. . . .

PHORIDS OR MANURE FLIES.

Several species of flies of the family *Phoridae* have been found in mushroom houses, including *Aphiochaeta albidihalteris* Felt, *A. pygmeae* Zett, and others. These small, active flies frequently occur in immense numbers about manure piles in warm weather, but some may occur there at any time of the year. Their bodies are shorter and heavier than the body of the *Sciarid* fly, and they are more active.

Description, Biology, and Injury. Phorids enter the mushroom houses either as larvae or in other stages in the manure; or as flies through the doors and ventilators. After the heat in the manure has decreased they generally are the first flies to appear and sometimes occur in very large numbers at the beginning of the season. Later they generally are replaced to a large extent by *Sciarid* flies.

Although they may occur in such large numbers, *Phorids* generally are less destructive than their numbers would indicate. As with the *Sciarids*, only the larvae cause injury. Two types of injury may be caused. Soon after the fall planting of the spawn the mycelium may fail to grow out of the spawn piece, which is gradually destroyed. Examination may show small white larvae eating the mycelium. These larvae differ from the *Sciara* larvae in that they have no black head, but show only black chitinous jaws, which work in and out of the fleshy pointed head and tear the mycelium. . . .

Control. In general the control methods are the same as for *Sciarids*. . . .

MUSHROOM MITE.

Several kind of mites have been found in mushroom houses but only two or three species cause injury to the crop. Of these, the Mushroom mite, *Tyroglyphus lintneri* Osborn, and the Long-legged mite, *Linopodes antennaepes* Banks are the most important. Gahm (1930b) also noted *Rhizoglyphus phylloxerae* as a pest of mushrooms. *Histiostoma* sp. attacks injured mushrooms.

Description and Biology. When the manure in the newly-filled beds reaches its top heat of 140° to 150°F., large numbers of very tiny white objects resembling round grains of sugar often may be seen crawling over the straw on the surface of the top beds. These are mushroom mites; if they are not killed by the heat or by a fumigation at this time, they may feed upon the mycelium later or come up on the casing soil and chew holes into the mushroom caps and stems. Because of their very small size they generally are overlooked by the grower, especially when they occur in the beds, yet they have been known to destroy the mycelium in the bed. . . .

The adults of the mushroom mite are less than half the size of an ordinary pin head. They are pearly white or yellowish white, resembling tiny drops of some opaque liquid, and have a number of long bristles projecting from the body. The mite has eight legs, which, together with the mouth parts, are flesh colored. The adults move slowly. . . .

Injury. All stages of the mites except the eggs and the hypopi can cause injury by feeding. Besides eating the mycelium in the beds, they sometimes chew holes in the surface of the stems and caps of the growing mushrooms. These holes appear dark within due partly to the large number of mites present, but chiefly to the excreta given off by them. These holes may be as large as the end of a finger; they ruin the mushroom for commercial use. Examination with a lens reveals that each hole contains smaller pits chewed into the sides, and in each pit are one or more mites. Small mushrooms are frequently hollowed out to a mere shell; these contain hundreds of individuals.

The mites are preyed upon by *Gamasid* mites, which are the swiftly running "red spiders" common on mushroom beds. Under certain conditions there *Gamasids* may keep the *Tyroglyphids* in check; but where the latter has appeared in injurious numbers on a bed, the "spiders" cannot be depended on to control them. A small orange-colored fly larva of the family *Cecidomyiidae* also feeds upon the mites, but is not common.

Control. Prevention is usually more effective than attempts to control after they have become abundant. Many of the mites in the manure of the top beds are killed by the extreme heat, but in the bottom beds the heat is frequently not even sufficient to drive them to the manure surface. Later the whole house may be re-infested from these lower beds. . . .

After the spawn is planted, sulphur cannot be used in the mushroom house, and the cyanide cannot be used strong enough to kill the mites without injuring the mushrooms. Attempts have been made to find some substance toxic to the mites, yet not injurious to the mycelium and mushrooms. Paradichlorobenzene will kill the mites if they are exposed to it for a sufficient period. Some success has been obtained by picking the good mushrooms, destroying the infested ones, then spreading muslin over the infested sections, broadcasting the paradichlorobenzene over the muslin and spreading newspapers over it. These are left on the beds for several days. Where left only a few hours to a day many of the mites recover within a few hours after removal of the muslin and papers. Where they are left on the bed too long, there is a slight retarding of mushroom growth. Therefore, if paradichlorobenzene is used, only a small section of a bed should be treated first to determine its effect upon both mites and mushrooms, and the time required. This method may not be practical where a whole house is infested. Caesar noted this measure in 1927.

Nicotine dusts and pyrethrum dusts have no value against Tyroglyphids. Sprays do not kill them unless such sprays contain oils. However, although oily fly-sprays will kill the mites if they hit them, they will turn the mushrooms brown and crack or deform them. Such sprays are for emergencies only. . . .

INSECT PREVENTION AND CONTROL.

Exactly why the beds cease to produce mushrooms does not appear to be fully understood but it is probably owing to the exhaustion of food material in the straw of the compost or to some excretion of the mushroom mycelium itself. A chief cause, and one which may not be so readily recognised by growers without experience is the damaging effect of larvae or maggots of flies and mites. These pests occur in houses more particularly at temperatures above 55°F. and breed exceedingly rapidly. From the eggs the flies lay, small white maggots emerge and prey upon the mycelium, buttons and large mushrooms. An attack of fly or mite if left unchecked can cause the cropping to come to an end before its full time has passed. When the small black flies (less than $\frac{1}{8}$-inch long) are observed, they should be killed off by fumigation with Auto-Shreds Fumigant or with " Black Arrow " Insect Dust.

When the beds have finished they should be removed from the house and may be used for manuring other crops, the compost being very valuable for this purpose. The material from old beds should not be used again for mushroom culture and it is useless to try to improve it in any way by incorporating with it fresh manure. All beds carted out for manuring purposes should be used on land from which casing soil will not be dug for at least six years, but this would not be the case if soil for casing beds was steamed as suggested before. The empty houses should be cleaned out thoroughly and the floors scraped. Full instructions for cleaning and disinfecting of mushroom houses, for preventing mushroom beds from becoming infected with Diseases and Pests, are given in our Leaflet No. 3. This leaflet will be gladly furnished upon receipt of application from growers.

A.—Mushroom attacked by *Mycogone perniciosa* in localized areas.

B.—Advanced stage of mycogone disease.

[*Facing p.* 6

DISEASES AND PESTS

There is no particular reason why clean crops of mushrooms should not be grown regularly provided good manure and clean soil are used and precautions to prevent infection and maintain clean conditions are taken, but the conditions of darkness under which mushrooms are grown are frequently allowed to obscure a lack of cleanliness both of the houses and the beds themselves.

A well kept mushroom house presents a delightful picture of orderliness and uniformity. Beds should be neat and well shaped, paths must be swept free from organic matter, all stumps must be removed immediately and the holes filled up with new casing soil, while the water tanks must be kept clean. Under such conditions, except by an unfortunate accident, diseases are unlikely to cause much damage, although the control of pests is still far from perfect. Untidiness and disorder are the certain precursors of trouble.

FUNGUS DISEASES

Mycogone

Mycogone or " bubbles " is a disease caused by the fungus *Mycogone perniciosa*. It has been recognized on the Continent for many generations and is probably the commonest mushroom disease. Although easily controlled it has been known to cause heavy losses.

The symptoms vary considerably. In slight attacks patches of white fungal growth appear on the gills in localized areas (Plate Xa, facing page 65), and the shape of the mushroom is not changed to any extent. In bad cases the entire mushroom is much swollen, and becomes a round warty mass of grotesque appearance (Plate Xb).

The stalk is greatly enlarged, the cap is almost indistinguishable and the whole structure is covered in a white fungal growth. Finally drops of watery exudate form on the surface and a bad odour is evolved.

Each diseased mushroom is a centre from which the disease may spread rapidly, for millions of spores are produced at the surface and these are readily distributed by insects, workers, tools, draughts, etc. As soon as a diseased mushroom appears it should be carefully dug out, taking away the entire stump and as much of the soil and compost as is necessary. It should be lifted carefully without undue shaking, laid in a paper lined receptacle placed close at hand, on the bed, and the whole burnt immediately. Care must be taken to impress upon the workers the ease with which the spores are shaken off and left on the bed to cause future damage. The hole left behind must be dusted thickly at once with hydrated lime and then filled up with new soil with which 20 per cent lime has been mixed. A little lime should also be dusted on the surface of the bed around the spot. Mycogone will not tolerate an excess of lime and can be controlled in this manner.

This disease is worst when the temperature is high and when the air is very moist and stagnant. Should the disease be serious, the air temperature should be reduced below 50° F. and the house allowed to dry out by withholding water and applying ventilation.

Serious outbreaks can be prevented by keeping a sharp look-out for the first signs of the disease and dealing with it *at once*, It is claimed by some that the brown strains of mushrooms are more resistant than the white strains to this disease. Treschow[1] in Holland has controlled outbreaks by spraying the beds with Bordeaux mixture 1–1–50 at the rate of 1 litre per square metre.

Truffle

The truffle disease due to *Pseudobalsamia microspora* Diehl and Lambert (Plate XI, facing page 72) was first discovered in this country by Williams, who published an account of it in 1936[2]. It had already been reported by Diehl and Lambert[3] as occurring in mushroom beds in several parts of the United States, and since then has been found in Denmark, but never in Great Britain until July, 1936, when it occurred in the mushroom shed at the Cheshunt Research Station, being introduced in imported casing soil.

Pseudobalsamia is not parasitic on the mushroom itself, but is a competitor in the beds and under favourable conditions it fills the compost so quickly and to such an extent that for all practical purposes the mushroom crop ceases.

Development of the truffle generally commences near the surface of the compost forming a dense mat of mycelial threads in which the fruiting bodies or ascocarps are produced in abundance. The ascocarps

[1] " *Champignondyrkning i Haver* " C. Treschow, Friesia 3: 189-196, 1946.

[2] " A disease of mushrooms new to Great Britain," *Gardeners' Chronicle*. Vol. c, No. 2591, p. 147, 22nd August, 1936.

[3] W. W. Diehl and E. B. Lambert, *Mycologia*. Vol. xxii, p. 223, 1930.

are cream to reddish brown in colour, subspherical to discoid in shape, and are lobed. In size they vary from a diameter of ⅛ in. to that of 1 inch. Infection is carried in the casing soil and this may be the chief means of transmission.

Beds which are too wet and too tight favour this fungus at the expense of the mushroom, while high temperatures and poor ventilation also increase its rate of growth.

All attempts to destroy the infection in the experimental beds at Cheshunt in 1936 failed, and this fungus is regarded as a distinct menace to mushroom work.

Williams concluded from its habit of growing near the surface of the beds that *Pseudobalsamia* is not likely to be found in subsoil to any extent, but the damage of which it is capable emphasises the importance of sterilizing all soil used for casing purposes. Kligman[1] says that the spores survived for 3 hours at 200° F., but were killed by 20 minutes at 250° F. Ordinary sterlization may not eliminate this fungus from the soil. He says also that the fungus does not spread to any extent in the soil and severe outbreaks indicate that the soil was heavily contaminated before use. The fungus can be controlled by keeping the temperature down to 60° F. and infected parts of the bed can be dried out to kill the mycelium and then brought into bearing again by watering.

Flock or Gill Mould

A white fungus *Cephalosporium lamellæcola* occasionally attacks a few isolated mushrooms on a bed, but it

[1] " Control of the truffle in beds of the cultivated mushroom." Kligman, A. M., *Phytopathology.* 34: 376–384, 1944.

need not be feared greatly because it rarely reaches serious proportions. As the name implies, it attacks the gills of the mushroom, binding them together with a white fungal growth (Plate XIIA). The cups and gills of infected mushrooms become very hard and stiff.

The disease is reputed to be favoured by high humidities and wetness of the casing soil.

Flock should not be confused with a genetic abnormality, Plate XIIB, in which the mushroom becomes extremely hard and tough and in which gill formation is so much retarded that each gill is represented by a ridge which is just perceptible. Where this abnormality occurs the percentage of mushrooms affected is usually so low that they are of no importance.

" Damping off "

The term " damping off " has been applied by Wood[1] to a disease of mushrooms in which they become brown and withered at all stages of growth.

Sometimes the young nodules are destroyed before they emerge above the casing soil, but usually the symptoms do not appear until the young buttons can be seen at the surface, when those which are infected turn brown and become pithy inside. In other cases, infection is revealed by the development of pithy mushrooms in which the stems are half-withered and brown inside.

Infection is contracted from the casing soil and is due to the presence of various species of Fusarium of

[1] Wood, F. C., " Studies on ' damping off ' of cultivated mushrooms and its association with Fusarium species," *Phytopathology*. Vol. 27, No. 1, pp. 85–94, 1937.

which the commonest are *F. oxysporum* and *F. martii.*

Another source of infection seems to be the water supply and mushroom growers should be careful to use clean water for all their work. That from shallow surface wells, ponds, streams, etc., may be infected.

This disease emphasizes again the advantage of using sterilized soil for casing purposes. Similar symptoms may be caused by disturbance of the mycelium when picking.

" *Cob-web* " *disease*

A disease which has been called " cob-web " disease by some growers is caused by *Dactylium dendroides* of which the perfect form is *Hypomyces rosellus,*

This fungus forms a greyish white cottony growth over and around the individual mushrooms, frequently enveloping and destroying them completely (Plate XIII). Infection is often present on beds from which the old stem bases have not been removed immediately and if much of this material lies on the surface the disease may be serious. Excessive humidity and cold conditions favour attack by this fungus.

In his *Handbook of the Large Fungi.* 1923, Rambottom indicates that this fungus attacks the gills of several fungi, including *Stereum hirsutum. Cantharellus aurantiacus* and others. *Cantharellus* grows wild in woods and pastures, a fact which confirms observations in mushroom sheds which suggest the transmission of this disease in casing soil.

Spraying isolated spots with a 2% solution of formaldehyde (1 part 40% formaldehyde in 49 parts water) has been suggested as a control, but it is a drastic measure and *should be tested on a very small scale* by anyone who wishes to try it.

White Plaster Mould.—White plaster mould is a serious disease of mushroom beds, for although it first appears on the surface of the casing soil as a thin dense layer suggestive of a heavy dusting of flour it also travels deeply into the bed and permeates it to the detriment of the mushroom mycelium. If left uncontrolled it may cause complete failure of the crop.

The fungus concerned is *Scopulariopsis* (*Monilia*) *fimicola* and if the white floury growth is examined under the microscope it will be found to consist of thin threads and millions of tiny spores produced in chains. These spores are spread easily by draughts and by the ordinary cultural operations.

In 1936, Williams,[1] working at the Cheshunt Research Station, discovered that *S. fimicola* would not grow on acid potato agar, pH $2 \cdot 8$–$4 \cdot 6$, while there was a pronounced increase in growth as the medium was made more and more alkaline. This discovery lead to practical measures being evolved for controlling this disease.

Observations in mushroom sheds indicate that it is not easy to detect white plaster mould until about twelve days after casing, when the fungus appears as small white areas on the surface. Closer examination reveals the fact that the fungus has spread to a greater extent in the compost below. If the diameter of the surface colony is 2 inches the areas below the casing soil may be 6 inches or more in width.

[1] Williams, P. H., *22nd Annual Report, Experimental and Research Station*. Cheshunt.

It was found that the fungus could be prevented from spreading through the bed by removing the infected material and filling the hole with acid peat saturated with acetic acid.

After successful trials on many nurseries it is possible to give the following recommendations.

(1) Remove carefully the infected casing soil, placing it without spilling in a paper lined box, near at hand. Then remove the surrounding casing soil until the compost below is uncovered slightly beyond the white infected area.

(2) Remove the white infected compost and fill up gradually with acid peat, moistening it thoroughly with dilute acetic acid applied from a small syringe or similar instrument. The acid solution is prepared by adding one part of 33% acetic acid to seven parts of water by volume (1 quart in 2 gallons). Sufficient acid must be added as will run into and wet some of the compost below and surrounding the peat.

(3) Finally re-cover with fresh casing soil.

This treatment must be applied as soon as the first infection appears on the surface, because in this way the infection is checked before it has made headway, which it does with great rapidity. Further, early treatment reduces the amount of compost which must be removed. In our experiments a large handful of peat was sufficient to fill loosely the hole in the bed.

Where shelves are used and the holes are deep it is advisable to place double thicknesses of newspaper on the surface of the bed beneath to prevent any acid from dripping through and injuring the mushrooms.

The results indicated that the fungus does not grow again in the acid treated areas, but if the patch treated

PLATE XI.

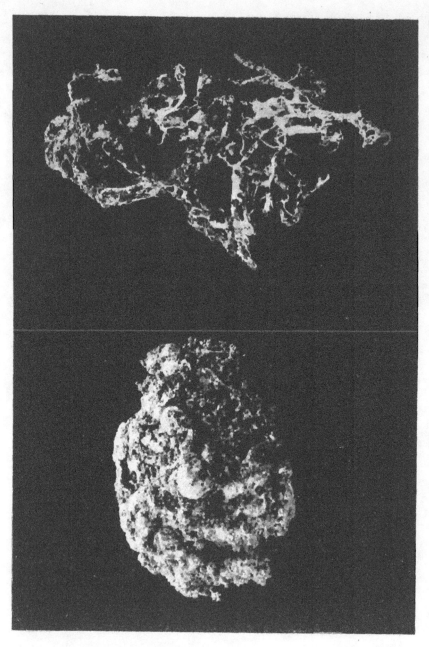

Pseudobalsamia microspora.

[*Facing p.* 72

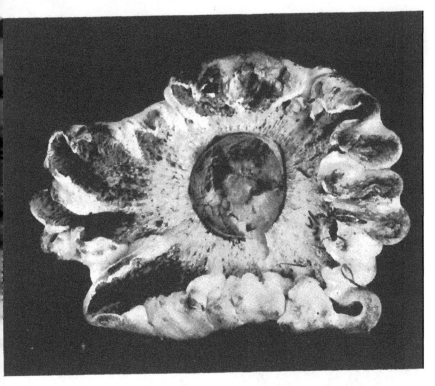

A.—Flock disease caused by *Cephalosporium lamellæcola.*

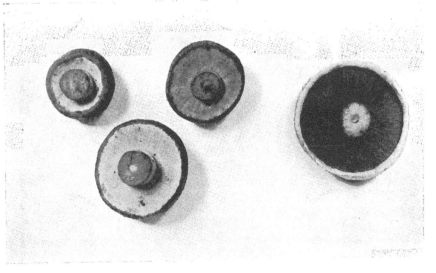

B.—Hard mushrooms with greatly reduced gills. Normal mushroom on right-hand side for comparison.

PLATE XIII.

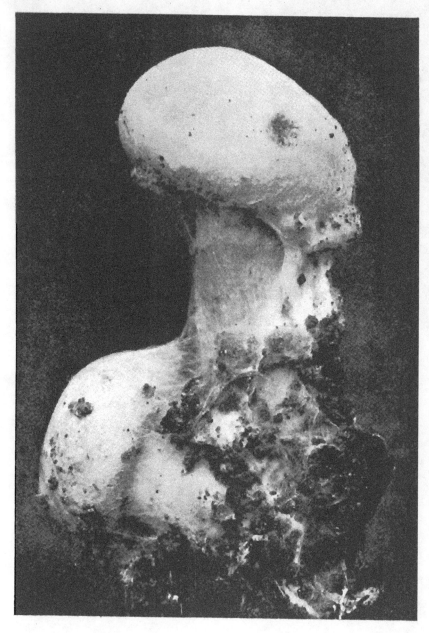

Cobweb disease, caused by *Dactylium dendroides*.

PLATE XIV.

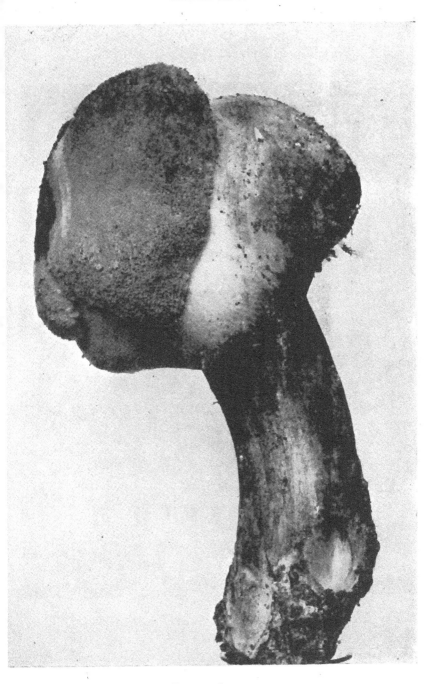

Rosecomb.

PLATE XV.

Mushroom attacked by *Verticillium malthousii*.

PLATE XVI.—*Mycetophilidae*

Sciara auripila Winn. Adult
female. × 16.

Sciara auripila Winn. Adult
male. × 16.

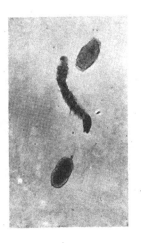

Eggs and young larva
of *Sciara auripila*
Winn. × 16.

Older larvae of
Sciara auripila
Winn. × 16.

Pupa of *Sciara
auripila*
Winn. × 16.

PLATE XVII.—*Phoridæ*

Megaselia halterata, Wood.
Adult female. ×16.

Megaselia halterata Wood.
Adult male. ×16.

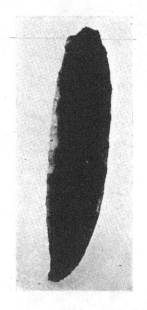

Megaselia halterata Wood.
Pupa. ×16.

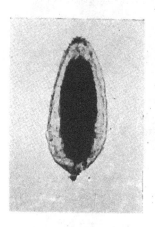

Megaselia halterata Wood.
Larva. ×16.

PLATE XVIII.—*Mushroom Mite*

Damage caused by Mushroom Mite.

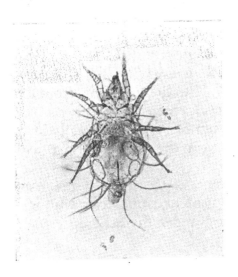

Tyroglyphus dimidiatus Herm.
Adult female. × 16.

does not cover the whole of the infected area the fungus may grow again around the treated portion, and this must be treated again.

In one case *Scopulariopsis fimicola* developed in three large sheds containing six double shevles.

The first treatment occupied one man and a boy the whole of one day. The second treatment attending to new outbreaks five days later was finished by midday, and the third treatment required only two hours' work to complete. After this no further infection was seen.

The yield from these beds totalled $2\frac{1}{2}$ lb. per square foot, and judging by recent experiences it would not have exceeded $\frac{1}{2}$ lb. per square foot if the outbreak of *S, fimicola* had not been checked.

When treating ridge beds, it will be borne in mind that the acid tends to gravitate downwards, and therefore the sponge of peat holding the acid will be placed at the highest point of the areas to be treated.

Scopulariopsis fimicola can be seen growing occasionally on the manure during the process of turning especially if the material is too dry. In such cases the dry places should be thoroughly wetted with water and the heaps made higher than usual (about 6 feet) to encourage fermentation. The addition of gypsum also helps to prevent the development of this fungus. Badly infected heaps have been cleaned successfully in this way and any outbreaks in the beds checked with peat and acetic acid.

Contamination of the floor of the house, and also shelves where used, must be dealt with effectively, and this is discussed under the heading " Site Contamination," page 79.

Brown Plaster Mould

This fungus *Papulospora byssina* is neither so common nor so serious as white plaster mould for it is restricted usually to the surface of the casing soil. The patches are white and resemble plaster at the beginning but they soon assume a light brown and then a cinnamon-brown colour. If examined with a lens the growth is seen to be composed of tiny spherical bodies or bulbils.

Brown plaster mould has long been known in this country and was observed by the authors in 1919. The best treatment for infected beds is removal of the growth by scraping away the surface of the casing soil.

Cap blemishes

(a) *Spots.*—Spotting of the cap is frequently associated with the presence of various bacteria of which *Bacillus tolaasi* has been proved pathogenic. Work with most other bacteria has not yielded positive results and much of the spotting is still unexplained.

(b) *Blotches.*—Light and dark brown blotches are often traceable to the use of insecticides such as nicotine. Often they are unavoidable and the loss in commercial value must be included in the cost of pest control.

Occasionally an impure water supply has led to injury of this kind; the trouble has ceased on using pure drinking water.

Usually, however, large discoloured areas are caused by damping with water too late in the day and leaving the ventilators closed afterwards. Houses should always be ventilated after damping the beds until such time as the moisture has dried off the surface of the mushrooms.

(c) *Cracking*.—Small cracks often develop on the caps, giving rise to a light and dark mottled appearance.

This seems to be caused by severe variations in atmospheric humidity, and over-dryness. In sheds it can be prevented by sprinkling the paths when necessary, but in unsuitable buildings the maintenance of sufficient moisture in the air is difficult. Draughts must be avoided and sheets of Hessian may be hung around the walls and doors and damped each morning.

Rose Comb

Occasionally mushrooms develop a curious form of hypertrophy in which numerous swellings appear on the cap (Plate XIV). As these develop, they open and produce gills. The resemblance to rose comb of poultry seems to have suggested the name.

In 1930, Lambert[1] noted the connection between this malformation and the presence of certain fumes, especially those from coal-oil, and mineral oils, and the use of sprays containing pyrethrum and kerosene. His views are generally accepted and appear to be confirmed by observations in this country.

Verticillium malthousii

This fungus may attack cultivated mushrooms with the production of a white fungal growth on the gills and stalk (Plate XV). Infection is followed by browning and death of the mushroom attacked and the early stages of the disease are not unlike those of mycogone but the rate of decay is not so rapid.

It was described by Ware in 1933 from cases he had

[1] Lambert, E. B., " Two new diseases of cultivated mushrooms," *Phytopathology*. Vol. 20, No. 11, pp. 917–19.

seen during the course of his investigations.

Xylaria vaporaria

This fungus is a serious competitor of the mushroom in beds to which it has gained entrance. The white mycelium grows rapidly through the compost taking the food necessary for the growth of the mushroom mycelium. When the fungus invades the casing soil it produces its black, fleshy resting bodies or sclerotia. These vary in length from anything up to 6 or 7 inches, are frequently branched, and have an objectionable odour.

This disease is extremely difficult to control, and it seems useless to attempt to pull the sclerotia out of the soil, because the real damage is caused by the mycelium in the compost.

The source of the fungus is not obvious although the casing soil is suspected.

Animal Pests

Of the several animal pests with which the mushroom grower may have to contend, the most important are certain fungus-gnats (Mycetophilidæ known as Sciarid flies) (Plate XVI). They measure $\frac{1}{16}$ to $\frac{1}{8}$ in. in length, are slender and vary in colour from light brown to black. They may, in general, be distinguished from other and non-injurious flies by their habit of running very actively over the surface of the casing soil and the wood-work of shelves, etc.

Though doubtless the grubs or chrysalids are sometimes introduced into the bed with the manure of which it is composed, it appears also likely that the adult flies are naturally present (even during the winter) in glasshouses which are used for mushroom culture.

The probability of the larvæ being present in casing soil, especially that which contains a good deal of organic matter, must not be overlooked.

When the beds are made and cased, the flies are at once attracted to the warm fermenting mass, and without delay lay their eggs in the casing soil.

The grubs of these flies are white, but with jet-black heads provided with powerful jaws. When fully grown, they attain a length of about ⅜ in. and turn to naked white chrysalids encased in a loose cocoon of soil.

The young grubs probably feed at first upon organic matter in the bed, but when older and present in large numbers, enter the stalks and caps of the mushrooms, which then become entirely " maggoty " in cases of severe infestation, which are frequent.

Phorid flies, Plate XVII, are also found in mushroom beds, chiefly during the summer. They are more active than the Sciarids and have shorter, thicker bodies. The larvæ are without black heads and are much thicker than those of the latter. Phorid flies usually lay their eggs at the base of the mushroom, and the larvæ on hatching tunnel up the stem into the cap.

Next in importance comes the Mushroom mite, the species most frequently met with being *Tyroglyphus dimidiatus* Herm. (= *longior* Gerv.).

This very small animal, about the size of a small pin's head when full-grown, is of a shining white appearance. Its extremely slow movements distinguish it from the larger and quickly moving mites nearly always present upon the beds: the latter are entirely predatory and may play quite an important part in checking outbreaks of injurious animals. It is practically certain that the *Tyroglyphus* mite is introduced in the straw from manure heaps which have not attained a high and even temperature through lack of care in turning, though there is an admitted possibility of the mites being carried by insects.

Under conditions favourable to them, the mites may permeate the manure of the entire bed, and migrate to the mushrooms, where they become packed between the gills. Sometimes they live in colonies upon the caps, upon which they cause large and deep brown wounds by their feeding (Plate XVIII).

A larger, very active pink mite with extremely long legs, *Eugamasus.* is sometimes found in large clusters upon the caps. When brushed off, no injury has been found, and it is doubtful if this mite is similar to species of Linopodes which cause severe injury to mushrooms in Canada and U.S.A.

Springtails (*Collembola*) make their appearance with great frequency upon mushroom beds, sometimes in such unbelievable numbers that the beds appear of a blue or purple colour, at least in large patches. These are very minute insects which have a habit of hopping. Their origin is quite obscure, for they will appear quite suddenly and again disappear for no apparent reason. Damage to the crop has been attributed to them, but in all instances so far examined, they have found their way into holes in cap and stem made by some other agency.

The grubs of certain " gall-midges " (*Cecidomyidæ*) occur in the compost below the casing soil. Minute red or pink grubs of *Mycophila* may to some extent feed upon the mycelium but any real injury from them is doubtful. Longer white grubs without black heads (cf. the Sciarid grub) belong to a midge known as

Miastor, These are definitely injurious, and are of some interest as they have never been known to transform to the adult fly, and produce young grubs inside themselves by a process of budding. The grub can withstand desiccation, and it is possible that they could be introduced in some types of spawn.

GENERAL CONTROL MEASURES FOR DISEASES, PESTS, AND OTHER CONTAMINATIONS

1. *Site Contamination*

Wherever mushrooms are cultivated certain contaminations, the nature of which is still unknown, pass into the soil beneath, with the result that succeeding crops of mushrooms become smaller and smaller until their cultivation ceases to be profitable. Although this fact has been known for years, it is not being recognized as it should and in consequence yields on many nurseries are lower than they ought to be.

The following examples may be quoted to illustrate the danger from this type of contamination.

(*a*) *Beds on the floor of glasshouses.*—In one case where mushrooms had not been grown previously the yield from 8 in. flat beds was 2·5 lb. per square foot during the winter. Tomatoes were grown during the summer and new flat beds put down in September for a second mushroom crop. The yield amounted to 1·2 lb. per square foot and during the next two winters it did not reach 1 lb. per square foot although in an adjacent block where mushrooms were being grown for the first time it averaged 2·2 lb. per square foot.

(*b*) *Ridge beds in the open.*—A farmer in the south of

England started the cultivation of mushrooms in standard ridge beds and obtained a yield of 1·9 lb. per square foot during the first crop. The following year, new beds were constructed on the old site and also on an equal area in an adjoining field. The yield was 1 lb. per square foot on the old site and 1·8 lb. per square foot on the new site. Next year these sites were covered with new beds and a new site also taken over in the normal extension of the work. The beds on the oldest site were a complete failure. They cropped for a few weeks and yielded less than 0·5 lb. per square foot. On the second year site the yield was 0·8 lb. per square foot, but in the new site it·was 1·8 lb. per square foot.

As the years passed, these results were repeated again and the grower was compelled to transfer the mushroom work to another farm.

(c) *Beds on the floor in wooden sheds.*—On the nursery of Mr. Harnett a new mushroom shed of the old type was built for 1932, and beds of the double ridge type were used.

The yields per square foot in succeeding years were as follows:—

	lb. per square foot.
1932	2·3
1932	0·5
1933	2·5
1933	2·4
1934	2·0
1934	2·5

After the failure of the second crop in 1932, plans were made to counteract the injurious effect of the base and being careful they were repeated before each new crop.

The site was scraped, swept clean, treated with sufficient formaldehyde to saturate the top 3 inches dusted with lime and covered with a layer of clean soil 2 inches deep. _

The result can be seen from the table on page 80.

Cases similar to the above are typical of what has happened in the mushroom industry and are a clear indication of the importance of the problem.

Proof that contaminated soil can be picked up and mixed with the manure has been obtained as follows:—

In an experiment the floor was covered with a layer of hydrated lime about $\frac{1}{4}$ in. thick and over it was spread a 2 in. layer of clean subsoil from an adjoining field. This was compacted by treading and the manure compost was brought in for the last two turns prior to bed making. When the beds had been made, the lime could be seen plainly in the ground beneath, showing that the top 2 inches of soil had been picked up unknowingly by the men and mixed with the compost. In this case the soil was new material and the crop was not injured in any way: the yield was 2·5 lb. per square foot.

Treatment

When ridge beds are made in the open it is easy to change the site and any expensive treatment of the ground may not be justified. It is, however, possible to renew the site each year by cleaning mechanically, treating with formaldehyde, covering the ground rather wider than the actual base of the beds with 2–3 inches of new soil.

In glasshouses, however, it is essential to clean the site before each new crop. Steam sterilization has not proved satisfactory and although the reason is not fully understood it may be connected with the production of ammonia or some of its derivatives.

The best treatment known so far is mechanical cleaning, and sterilization of the site with formaldehyde. For this purpose 1 gallon of 40% formaldehyde is mixed with 49 gallons of water and applied to 60 square yards for the purpose of saturating the top 3 inches of soil. Five to seven days later a covering of clean subsoil is placed over the site to a depth of 2 inches and after consolidating it, the compost is brought in and the beds made in the usual manner. This treatment has proved effective whenever it has been tried.

2. *Cleaning and disinfection of houses, sheds, etc.*

In mushroom work, extreme cleanliness is essential. Some growers may consider that the methods to be recommended are much too expensive but experience has shown, only too clearly, that they are necessary to success.

When the crop is finished the first task is to destroy as many insects as possible by the process of cyaniding, because any pests taken outside will continue to breed and will re-enter the houses when the next crop is developing. This is done by fumigating the houses with hydrogen cyanide and the most convenient method of doing this is to use proprietary cyaniding preparations which gives off the gas when exposed to air and moisture.

The cubic capacity of the building is calculated by measuring in feet the length, width, height to the eaves and height to the ridge. The average height is obtained by adding the height of the ridge to the height of the eaves and dividing by two. The cubic capacity is obtained by multiplying the length by the width and the product by the average height.

$$\text{Average height} = \frac{\text{height to eaves} + \text{height to ridge.}}{2}$$

Cubic capacity = length × width × average height.

Having calculated the cubic capacity of the house the necessary amount of the proprietary cyaniding powder, as advised by the manufacturer, should be sprinkled on the pathways of the houses.

This must be done by a responsible person and the houses locked until the following morning when they should be opened and thoroughly aired before anyone enters, for hydrogen cyanide is extremely poisonous to man. *For this reason it must not be used in buildings which adjoin or form part of any human habitation.*

If any serious disease has occurred in the beds, they should be soaked thoroughly with formaldehyde (1 gallon 40% formaldehyde in 49 gallons water) before removal, to prevent infection spreading outside, but when disease is absent, the beds can be taken out and stacked in some remote part of the nursery. When the mycelium is dead, the spent material may be used on certain crops, although for others it should be sterilized first. Expert advice should be sought before using it.

The next step is to sweep the houses, shelves, etc., clean and then thoroughly soak everything with formaldehyde, finally shutting up the houses and maintaining a temperature of 90° F. if possible for 48 hours. Afterwards the houses should be ventilated and washed down thoroughly when the vapours have escaped.

In ordinary houses, where beds are to be made on the soil floor, this should be treated for site contamination. In the case of shelves, the blow lamp must be used.

Too much emphasis cannot be laid upon the benefit which results from the blow lamp treatment, because in many cases it has been the means of growing successful crops after a series of failures. Every grower who specializes in shelf beds cannot afford to be without one or more blow lamps. For a preliminary trial, a painter's blow lamp may be used but the work is slow and larger instruments are now available.

The flame is moved quickly over the wood of the shelves and uprights so that any projecting fibres are singed but the surface of the timber is not burnt.

Some growers may wonder why the blow lamp must be used when so much care has been taken in applying formaldehyde, but until the nature of the contamination is fully understood an answer cannot be given. Experiments have shown, however, that the blow lamp treatment cannot be omitted.

3. *Fumigation at peak heat*

One great advantage of the shelf system is that the moisture content of the compost can be reduced if necessary by increasing the temperature of the shed before the beds have been compacted, and also that many of the insects present can be driven to the surface and destroyed by fumigation.

When the compost is first placed on the shelves loosely it is about 14 inches deep, for this amount will ultimately compress down to 8 inches. After the house is closed down the temperature is gradually increased up to 90° F. If the compost is very wet the ventilators can be left open for a day or two until it has dried out sufficiently. Then the house is closed down and the temperature of the compost rises to 125°–130° F. When the temperature remains constant for two consecutive days " peak heat " has been reached, many flies have hatched out and most living creatures have come to the surface of the beds.

The shed is then fumigated with cyanide as described in connection with the cleaning and disinfection of houses. Next day the houses are opened to eliminate the poisonous gas before anyone is allowed to enter unless supplied with a suitable gas-mask.

4. Pest control during the growing season.

It is essential that control measures should be applied immediately the presence of a pest is observed since it is exceedingly difficult to eliminate several of the most serious pests of mushrooms once the beds have become invaded.

Regular dusting with DDT or pyrethrum dusts or treatment with DDT aerosols or smoke generators will destroy adult Sciarid flies. The larvæ within the beds are not destroyed by this treatment consequently if the beds become infested with larvæ it is necessary to treat them with nicotine solution.

For this purpose 10–15 fluid ounces of commercial

(95–98%) nicotine to every 100 gallons of water is recommended.

The day before the nicotine is to be applied the beds should be watered lightly with a solution of common salt (small tablespoon to 2 gallons of water). This brings many larvæ etc., to the surface and exposes them to the nicotine solution.

The nicotine is watered or sprayed carefully over the beds to wet the casing soil only. This treatment may be supplemented by trapping the adult flies upon white paper or pieces of glass smeared with a strong adhesive such as tangle-foot.

The flies are also attracted by light. If windows are present they can be uncovered for an hour each day, and cotton wool soaked in nicotine solution placed on the sills. The flies go to the windows and are killed by the nicotine fumes. Alternatively powerful lights may be installed in the shed and trays of paraffin or weak nicotine solution placed beneath to trap the flies.

The Mushroom mite *Tyroglyphus dimidiatus* is not easy to control. Where the mites exist at the surface of the beds they can be destroyed by means of a painter's blow-lamp, because, if carefully used, the surface can be burnt without injury to the mycelium below. This treatment has proved successful in many serious attacks and obviously it must be applied between flushes when only a few mushrooms exist here and there.

Pure grade 16 naphthalene can be used effectively, scattering it on the paths only at the rate of 4 oz. per 1,000 cubic feet. It should be applied between flushes, because the mushrooms may absorb some slight flavour, and they may also be disfigured by brown patches. By choosing the correct time, however, the maximum killing effect can be obtained with a minimum of damage. The treatment is one which can be recommended.

Woodlice may be trapped in pots and boxes containing hay, which are laid on the surface of the beds. Mangels, cut in half with the cut surface laid against the sides of the beds, are also useful traps.

Woodlice may be controlled by dusting the beds and paths of the house with DDT dusts.

Regular treatment of the beds with dilute salt solution is a valuable method for keeping the cultures healthy. It stimulates growth and seems to keep down diseases and pests. If the timber of boards and uprights are sawn, they should be treated by painting or spraying the surface with a good brand of creosote for it will soak into the timber and acts as a deterrant to flies of all kinds and does not harm the mushrooms. Planed wood is not suitable for the creosote does not soak in and the surface remains wet for a considerable time. This treatment has been highly effective at Cheshunt since 1937.

5. *General hygiene*

Those who contemplate the cultivation of mushrooms would be well advised to take full heed of the disastrous effect of contaminations of every kind, to study their natures so far as they are known and to learn the sources from which they are likely to arise.

The first essential is a clean start. Those who are sufficiently fortunate in possessing one of the latest sheds will have no difficulty in starting each crop under clean conditions if they will follow the recommendations outlined previously. In the case of glasshouses and improvised structures over a soil floor the inside of the superstructure can be cleaned effectively but the soil is a breeding-ground for insects and also carries site contaminations unless treated suitably.

The compost itself may contain harmful insects and fungi unless it has been thoroughly fermented at the correct temperatures.

The casing soil, once disregarded as a source of diseases and pests, has proved an important source of infection. The use of sterilized soil eliminates this source of contamination and is preferred.

The water supply can also be a source of infection and must be taken into serious consideration. Clean, deep wells, or company's water of drinking quality should be used whenever possible. All water tanks should be thoroughly cleansed by scrubbing and treatment with formaldehyde.

Contamination can also be introduced by the workers from infected areas, on shoes, barrows, tools, etc. *No one should be allowed to stand on the side-boards of the bottom shelves to inspect the top shelves.* Disease has been carried in this way.

Expert advice should be sought immediately a pest or disease attack commences, unless the grower is conversant with the trouble and the methods adopted for controlling it. Diseases and pests which defy control when they have become well established can often be controlled quite easily at the commencement of an attack.

Brown plaster mould and other superficial growths can be checked readily by careful and regular brushing of the surface of the casing soil. They should not be allowed to accumulate. All diseased and broken mushrooms and stalks must be removed at once and the holes filled up with new casing soil, to which lime is added if the nature of the disease demands it. If this is not done, they form excellent breeding centres from which diseases and pests will spread rapidly. Care must be taken not to drop any infected pieces either in the beds or paths. They must be taken away at once and either soaked in formaldehyde or burned. Cleanliness outside the houses is equally important, and applies to fields of ridge beds or any form of culture.

When a serious disease develops in a portion of a bed, it is often advisable to soak it with a 2 per cent solution of emulsified cresylic acid prior to removing it for sterilization or destruction outside, because in some cases it is best to sacrifice a portion of the crop to save the remainder.

It must be remembered that mushroom diseases are encouraged by high temperatures and excessive dampness, and in consequence these should be avoided.

Conclusion

While the cultivation of mushrooms cannot be regarded as a carefree process there is no reason why it should not become a good source of income provided careful attention is paid to all the essential details. The scientific principles which underlie it are still not fully understood but when the knowledge has been wrested from Nature the maximum crops of to-day will no doubt become the average of to-morrow.

Diseases and Competitors

Complete or partial failure of the mushroom crop may be the result of faults in cultural methods, disease, competition with other fungi, or attack by pests.

Diseases are caused by infection of the mushroom with other fungi, with bacteria, or even perhaps with virus. The most common of the disease-causing fungi are *Mycogone perniciosa* (White Mould or Bubbles), *Verticillium malthousei* and *V. psalliotae* (Verticillium Disease), *Dactylium dendroides* (Cobweb Disease); *Mycogone rosea* has been reported on mushrooms in England once or twice in recent years though it was discovered in France half a century ago. Among bacteria, *Pseudomonas tolaasi* is considered as the cause of Brown Blotch, a spotting of the cap, while other species are found associated with the pitting of the cap. In the U.S.A., it is thought likely that Mummy Disease is due to infection by a virus.

The most dangerous known competitors (weeds) in mushroom beds are probably *Pseudobalsamia microspora* (Truffle) and *Fusarium* spp. (Damping-off). Others include *Papulaspora byssina* (Brown Plaster Mould),

Scopulariopsis (Monilia) fimicola (White Plaster Mould), *Xylaria vaporaria* (Mushroom Bed Sclerotium), *Clitocybe dealbata* and *Clitopilus cretatus*. The last three have become of much less importance since hygienic measures were adopted generally by mushroom growers.

Except for *Fusarium*, these mushroom bed invaders have fairly prominent forms by which they can be recognized by the unaided eye. It must be remembered, however, that in the same way that the material of mushroom beds encourages the growth of the cultivated mushroom, so it is suitable for the growth of many (perhaps hundreds) of other fungi. Most of these are not easily noticed and presumably do not offer serious competition with the mushroom. On the other hand, it is not unlikely that a number of these invisible moulds sometimes interfere with mushroom growth and are even responsible for many unexplained failures. Much investigational work requires to be done before the natural inhabitors of compost and soil can be identified and their role known. Two which have been suspected of interfering with mushroom growth are *Myceliophthora lutea* and a species of *Sporendonema* (Red Geotrichum) with red-coloured spores. The former has been considered responsible for the trouble known as Mat Disease in U.S.A. and is possibly also one of the fungi to which the name of *Vert-de-gris* (or Verdigris) has been given.

Damage to mushrooms sometimes occurs through non-parasitic agencies. Mineral oils or the fumes resulting from their combustion, unsuitable grades of creosote, or inadequately-dried creosote, and improper use of some phenolic disinfectants may cause a deformity known as Rose Comb (Plate XVI). The caps become distorted, with pink gill-like outgrowths on top of the cap or in clefts. In this connection it is interesting to note that similar outgrowths of the cap of a species of *Coprinus* (Ink Cap) were produced by exposing to a current of air (Keyworth (1942)). Draughts in mushroom houses should be avoided.

Accounts are given in the following pages of the most important diseases and competitors of mushrooms.

DISEASES

White Mould (*Mycogone perniciosa*)

White Mould, often called Bubbles, may appear at any time after the commencement of cropping. A close white fungal growth appears over part or the whole of the mushroom and although deformity does not invariably occur, it is typical that whole clumps of young mushrooms grow into shapeless masses (Plate XVI). If a single diseased mushroom is examined it will be seen that the stalk is short and much swollen and that the cap is scarcely developed. After being in this condition for a few days, affected mushrooms quickly decay and emit a disagreeable odour. Droplets of brown liquid often appear on the surface and these have prompted the name " Bubbles ".

There has, for many years, been a belief in this country that certain strains of brown mushroom are immune to the disease, and Treschow (1942-43) found immunity in a brown variety in Denmark, but more recently it has been found that brown mushrooms may be attacked in Denmark.

Mycogone rosea may occasionally be found infecting a few mushrooms in which it causes a browning of the cap to a depth of about ¼ in. This disease, however, is not of economic importance.

Control

High temperatures at cropping-time favour infection by White Mould which has an optimum of 75° F. Near 50° F., spread is likely to be slow. Thus, as soon as symptoms have appeared, the temperature of the house should be reduced to 55° F. or lower. *M. perniciosa* produces myriads of spores and these rapidly disseminate the mould to all parts of the bed. The spread of *M. perniciosa* has sometimes been prevented by spraying the bed between flushes with home-made Bordeaux mixture.* In recent trials fungicides containing thiram and zineb have given good control of Bubbles (1 lb. per 100 gal. water, spraying 1 gal. on 50–100 sq. ft before fruiting or between flushes).

M. perniciosa is a mould common on "wild" outdoor mushrooms and its introduction to mushroom houses seems to be most frequently with unpasteurized casing soil. Once it has entered a grower's premises, however, it is likely to cause infection to successive crops unless strict measures of hygiene are adopted. Pasteurization of the casing soil by heat or by formalin is a means of prevention (see pp. 53–55).

Infected mushrooms and a surrounding 6-in. margin of the bed should be sprayed with 5 per cent formalin to kill the fungus (see Plate XXII). The diseased mushrooms should be removed after spraying, and burned. Watering or picking should be deferred until this has been done.

Verticillium Disease (*Verticillium malthousei* and *V. psalliotae*)

Verticillium Disease characteristically causes irregular, light brown, slightly sunken spots on the caps of mushrooms. A white or light grey mould may develop over the button (Plate XVII) but the growth is not as close or abundant as that of *Mycogone perniciosa*, with which *Verticillium* sp. should not be confused. Both moulds can grow on the gills and both cause distortion, but with *Verticillium* the infected buttons become dry and do not produce an offensive odour. There is a tendency for the stems to split in the manner shown in Plate XVII.

Control

Verticillium Disease is most damaging in houses where the temperature and the relative humidity are high and where ventilation is poor. Under these conditions, spores are produced in abundance ; spread is not only by air currents but also by insects. The treatment of Verticillium Disease is similar to that recommended for White Mould, with emphasis on improved ventilation. Atmospheric humidity should be reduced to 88 per cent or below ; if temperature alone is reduced it may be found that the relative humidity will be increased with a corresponding stimulus to spread

---

* To make 3 gallons of Bordeaux mixture, dissolve 1 oz. granular copper sulphate (bluestone) in ½ pint warm water and when cool stir this into 23½ pints cold water into which 1 oz. finely powdered hydrated lime has previously been shaken. Apply at the rate of 1½ pints per sq. yd.

of the disease. All infected buttons must be removed from the house and burnt ; spraying the casing with home-made Bordeaux mixture should help to reduce spread.

There is good evidence that *Verticillium* sp. are introduced in the first instance with the casing soil. Pasteurization with heat or with 5 per cent formalin is the best method of avoiding infection.

Mushrooms infected with *Verticillium*, and a surrounding 6–in. margin of the bed should be sprayed with 5 per cent formalin to destroy the disease fungus. The mushrooms should then be carefully removed and burned. This should be done before watering the bed or picking.

Cobweb Disease (*Dactylium dendroides*)

On beds infected with Cobweb Disease a rapidly growing downy or fluffy mould creeps over the surface of the bed covering single mushrooms or whole clumps with a cobweb-like mycelium. The colour is white with often a rosy tint. Mushrooms, when covered, completely rot away. Spores are disseminated by currents of air, by watering, and by human and insect agencies.

D. dendroides, like *Mycogone* and *Verticillium*, thrives best where temperature and moisture are high, but will progress under most conditions of commercial mushroom growing.

Control

There is good evidence that casing soil is the main means by which *D. dendroides* is introduced on to a mushroom grower's premises in the first instance. Pasteurization with heat or with 5 per cent formalin is the best method of avoiding infection.

Mushrooms infected with Cobweb Disease should be formalin-sprayed as for *Verticillium*.

Brown Blotch or Bacterial Spot (*Pseudomonas tolaasi*, and probably other species of bacteria).

Brown Blotch and Bacterial Spot are names given to a super-ficial spotting of mushroom caps (Plate XVIII). The spots, at first yellow, become brown. The source from which the bacteria come is unknown, but it is certain that the blotch is worse in the presence of abundant moisture and can occur even when atmospheric temperatures are fairly low. The spotting is favoured by globules of water remaining on the caps. Sufficient ventilation should therefore be given to dry the mushrooms rapidly after watering, although draughts should not be maintained long enough to dry the beds.

Control

If Bacterial Spot is severe, an application to the bed of home-made Bordeaux mixture between flushes may reduce the infection.

Bacterial Pit

Small pits or depressions may sometimes appear over the surface of the caps. These pits frequently contain glistening masses of bacteria to which the damage has been attributed by some workers. Atkins (1948) has remarked that pits are often found just below the surface of the cap into which the covering wall ultimately collapses.

Mummy Disease

Tucker and Routien (1942) have described Mummy Disease as being prevalent in parts of the U.S.A. It has some similarity to Damping-off but no causal organism has been discovered. From its proved contagious or infectious nature, however, these investigators consider that a virus might be responsible.

Where infection has occurred the mushrooms develop long slender stalks and small tilted caps, or growth is arrested in the button stage and the tissue becomes grey or brown, and dry, spongy, and mummified. Cream strains are liable to a wet rot. The disease spreads through beds at the rate of about 1 ft. in 24 hours and once a patch is affected, normal mushrooms are rarely produced on it.

The disease does not readily spread from bed to bed, but infection is likely to be present 4-6 ft. in advance of the youngest visibly diseased mushrooms and its progress may be checked by arranging narrow trenches across the beds 6-8 ft. in advance of the visibly affected margin. It is thought that Mummy Disease is introduced with the casing soil in the first instance and there is evidence that it may be eliminated from this by pasteurization with steam or with certain chemicals such as formalin.

Similar symptoms have occasionally been seen in this country, but no evidence has been obtained that a virus was responsible, and it seemed more likely that some agent in the soil was the cause.

COMPETITORS

Truffle (*Pseudobalsamia microspora*)

Truffle is not, in spite of the name, the well-known edible truffle but a member of an allied group. After the compost and the casing have been filled with mushroom mycelium, the spores of *P. microspora* germinate and a cream-coloured mycelium overruns the already occupied bed. Cream-coloured fruiting bodies (Plate XVIII) appear often in great abundance within the compost and the casing soil ; these later become reddish brown. They are typically sub-spherical in shape, ⅓ in.-1 in. in diameter, and irregularly lobed ; their appearance has been likened to calves' brains. They are formed on the surface of the bed or in cavities in the compost.

Each fruiting body contains large numbers of spores which are released when the outer covering decays. The spores themselves may then be distributed in the house or elsewhere on the premises and contaminate the beds of future crops. The spores require a temperature of about 60° F. or more in order to germinate and little or no growth appears to take place until the alkalinity of the compost is reduced by the running of mushroom spawn in it. Spores of *P. microspora* are extremely difficult to kill with normal fungicides or with heat. They have survived a temperature of 180° F. for five hours.

It is considered that as a rule the initial outbreaks of Truffle are due to the presence of spores in the soil and that there is little spread from infected patches to uninfected parts of the same bed or from one bed to another. Once the fruiting bodies have decayed, however, there is a risk, when emptying the beds, that compost or casing soil for subsequent beds will become contaminated.

Control

If Truffle is discovered in small patches during an early stage of development, saturation of the sites with formalin may kill the fungus before spore formation occurs. Complete removal of the debris from the house is important and a spraying with formalin may kill any mycelium which might be residual in crevices. After a bed has been infected, persistence of the fungus in bed-boards is a likely source of reinfection and even strong disinfectants do not appear to be successful in killing it. There is some evidence that a lining of bituminized sisal paper to separate the infected boards from new beds will help to reduce infection from this source. As treatment of the soil at normal pasteurization temperatures does not kill the spores, a new source of soil is to be recommended if an outbreak has occurred. Where Truffle has been troublesome, the grower would be well advised to attempt to keep the house at a temperature below 60° F. throughout the whole of a few successive crops, so that the spores have little opportunity to germinate while mushroom spawn is running.

Damping-off (*Fusarium oxysporum* and *F. martii*)

Damping-off is due to the toxic effect of species of *Fusarium* on mycelium in the bed. There may be little or no mushroom production, or after a good first flush the crop may degenerate into small, withered, brown and undeveloped buttons which remain on the beds without rotting. In a normal or heavy crop, some of the mushrooms are found to be dry and pithy inside the stalk ; they are of pith-like texture and usually brown internally. Mushrooms of the brown variety have the caps shining as though burnished whereas healthy ones show a matt surface. Sometimes the trouble is localized in patches or is confined to one or more beds in a house.

Control

When *Fusarium* has infected a section of bed, no known treatment will control it. Once it has appeared in a house the woodwork may become contaminated and the disease may pass to successive crops unless rigorous steps of elimination are adopted. The treatment of woodwork with creosote has been found efficacious in killing *Fusarium*, and this practice has long been used by many growers.

Harmful species of *Fusarium* are probably first introduced with casing soil from which they can be removed by pasteurization with steam.

White Plaster Mould (*Scopulariopsis fimicola*, syn. *Monilia fimicola* and *Oospora fimicola*)

The name " White Plaster " is derived from the mould's appearance on the bed as scattered plaster or lime. There is good evidence that White Plaster Mould is usually brought into the house with compost and copious development of mycelium occurs after the beds have been made up. If casing is not carried out fairly soon, white patches of the sporing fungus appear on the surface, but more often the patches are not seen until the fungus has passed through the casing soil and appeared as a patch of "plaster" on the surface.

White Plaster Mould is favoured by alkaline conditions and, unlike Truffle, does damage by occupying the compost before the mushroom mycelium has spread. This disease caused substantial losses to mushroom growers before the addition of gypsum to composts was general. Since then the losses appear to have been reduced to small proportions either by the suppression of the fungus or by a mitigation of its effect on crop production.

Brown Plaster Mould (*Papulaspora byssina*, syn. *Myriococcum praecox*)

Brown Plaster Mould is first seen as fluffy or matted patches on the compost. Within a few days the centre of each patch turns brown, with the formation of a powdery mass of granules (bulbils) which has the appearance of sand but is soft and not gritty when rubbed between thumb and finger. When the bed is cased the fungus penetrates the soil and forms new patches on the surface. For a time these are white, then brown with a white fringe, but finally they become completely brown and powdery. Mushrooms may appear on patches of bed which have been infected by Brown Plaster Mould, but they appear later than those on the rest of the bed and the yield is invariably reduced.

Brown Plaster Mould is almost always introduced into the house with compost rather than with soil and there is good evidence that contaminated composting ground is one of the most regular sources of reinfection. No treatment can be recommended for beds already infected but if general hygiene and cleanliness are observed on the composting site, which should have a smooth cement floor, there is every prospect of eliminating the mould ; should it still persist, then another composting site, as remote as possible from the offending one, should be used.

Insect and Other Pests

A considerable number of insect and other pests are known to attack mushrooms but there are relatively few which are of great importance when the crop is grown in modern mushroom houses, although at times most growers sustain appreciable loss from them. Most of the creatures concerned are very small and difficult to identify with certainty ; therefore the destructive species can only be differentiated from harmless or even beneficial ones by careful examination.

Growers are often concerned at the large number of flies and mites commonly seen around compost heaps and on beds, fearing that serious attacks on mushrooms will result, but this is by no means always so. Stable manure is attractive to a great many forms of animal life, because directly or indirectly, it provides food for them. It is, for instance, a substance on which many fungi grow, so that creatures which feed upon fungi might be expected to congregate on it. On the other hand, it attracts many small forms of life that require only decomposing animal and vegetable refuse and are not directly concerned with fungi. The fungus feeders may eventually attack mushrooms but the others may be disregarded. Finally, as usually happens, numbers of carnivorous and parasitic mites and insects congregate in any such medium, because it supports a population of creatures on which they prey.

The pests may be roughly classified into three groups:

Creatures normally inhabitating buildings and situations used for growing mushrooms

Creatures that may be introduced with manure, soil, or straw litter used for covering beds

Creatures that are specific to fungi—that is, they are attracted to growing mycelium or mushrooms. Such creatures, although they may occur in manure, may also be attracted into mushroom houses even if they are not brought in with manure.

CREATURES NORMALLY INHABITING BUILDINGS AND SITES

In nearly all instances these are not insects, but other animals which commonly frequent semi-dark, moist situations, especially where there is old wood and brickwork in which they can shelter, and an accumulation of organic debris. They appear to feed chiefly upon this organic matter or upon the fungi growing on it, but they turn their attention to mushroom beds, for from the very nature of its composition, a prepared mushroom bed provides them with suitable conditions and food supply. On the other hand, these animals are not usually numerous in the compost itself when it is brought in, so that unless they are already present in the building, they are not likely to become sufficiently prevalent to be harmful. It follows then, that the repair of structural woodwork and masonry, and attention to general hygiene are essential for successful control; unless this is done, the results obtained from the application of other measures may be disappointing.

Woodlice

The familiar "pill-bugs" or "monkey-peas", as woodlice are called in some parts of the country, normally inhabit decaying wood, and several species—such as *Oniscus asellus* L., *Porcellio scaber* Latr., and *Armadillidium vulgare* (Latr.)—have been recorded as injurious to mushrooms. Some roll themselves up into a ball when disturbed, but in others this characteristic is not apparent. They spoil the appearance of mushrooms by chewing holes in the caps. This damage is done at night, for they hide in the day beneath the straw covering on beds, or in crevices in soil or walls.

Control

When attacking ordinary glasshouse crops, woodlice can be controlled with DDT or by using poison baits composed of 1 lb. Paris green to 25 lb. coarse bran, or 1 lb. Paris green to 56 lb. dried blood. The use of an arsenical poison like Paris green is undesirable, however, on mushroom beds, but an effective control can be obtained by the use of pyrethrum insecticides which have the advantage of being non-poisonous to human beings. Pyrethrum in dust form is particularly useful, since it can be blown into crevices where woodlice hide, and scattered lightly over beds and along the bases of walls. Woodlice walking over the dust are killed, and attacks can be kept in check in this way. Five per cent DDT or BHC dusts are also useful.

Slugs

Slugs need damp conditions, and most frequently attack beds near the walls of a house but they are particularly important on outdoor beds. They eat large pieces out of the caps and stalks, sometimes devouring quite half a mushroom. The file-like " tongue " with which slugs tear off their food gives the attacked mushrooms the appearance of having been eaten by rats or mice. The presence of slugs is, however, generally betrayed by slime marks.

Control

Hand collection is the most effective method of dealing with attacks, for slugs are usually few in number and large enough to be seen easily. Moreover, they are so fond of mushrooms that they eat them in preference to some poison baits. A few collecting visits at night with the aid of a good light is sufficient to keep attacks in check.

Careful use of metaldehyde bait is worth consideration. A suitable mixture can be made by incorporating 1 part by weight powdered metaldehyde with about 50 parts bran. The mixture should be placed in small heaps, not more than half a handful each, the heaps being covered with pieces of tile or board sufficiently raised to allow slugs to crawl beneath. Metaldehyde is poisonous to human beings, so the bait heaps should never be placed on beds, but along the bases of walls. In all probability a cellar or building can be cleared of slugs most effectively before mushroom beds are laid down, though measures might need to be more protracted out of doors. One small heap of bait every three or four yards should be sufficient.

Millepedes

Millepedes are elongated creatures with very numerous legs, and many of the species curl up into a spiral, spring-like form when disturbed. Three species (*Blaniulus guttulatus* (Bosc.), *Choneiulus palmatus* Nemec., and *Cylindroiulus britannicus* (Ver.)) are known to injure mushrooms. They are all rather less than $\frac{1}{4}$ in. long when adult, but immature forms are much smaller. *B. guttulatus* is very pale in colour, with a row of red spots along each side ; the others are pale fawn or brown, with a row of darker brown spots along each side. *C. britannicus* is more than twice as stout as the other two. Injury occurs at ground level and takes the form of holes eaten in the stalks, sometimes extending deeply into the tissue. Crops growing in glasshouses seem to be most frequently attacked.

Control

Damage can largely be prevented by the use of nicotine sprays, or by dusting or spraying with BHC or DDT.

Springtails

The minute insects called springtails, which are entirely wingless, derive their name from their marked power of jumping. They normally live in soil, particularly if it has a high humus content, and, like millepedes, frequently occur in glasshouses, where severe attacks sometimes occur. It is not improbable, however, that under some conditions they are present in appreciable numbers in the manure itself (see Plate XIX).

By far the most injurious species is *Achorutes armatus* (Nic.), a tiny insect about $\frac{1}{16}$ in. long, which varies from silver-grey to dark bluish-black in colour. Another species (*Proisotoma minuta* (Tullb.)) is often found in smaller numbers. Masses of the insects are sometimes to be seen on beds or assembled near walls, and they are often referred to by growers as "gunpowder mites". They are able to penetrate into the beds, where they attack the spawn and destroy the young buttons just as they are breaking through the casing soil. In extreme cases, total failure of crop may result, but this is rare and the more usual type of injury takes the form of small holes bored into the stalks, which connect with tunnels extending deeply into the mushroom. These may be continued right through the cap, and splitting of the stalk often results. The tunnels are usually drier than those made by fly maggots and, of course, where springtails are entirely responsible for the injury, maggots are absent.

Control

Dusting the beds before and after casing, with BHC as recommended for fly control, together with routine smoking or dusting with BHC should prevent trouble. Once an attack has been allowed to develop, it is difficult to control, and spraying with BHC, nicotine, or TEPP should be tried. Nothing is known about the conditions that induce the very severe attacks which sometimes occur, but possibly the state of the compost is largely responsible. Springtails seem to be killed readily by the high temperatures reached during fermentation and, according to observations made in the U.S.A., they are more susceptible in this respect than many other insects.

CREATURES THAT MAY BE BROUGHT IN

When true subsoil is used for casing, it may be assumed that few or no insects are introduced with it, for such forms of life are rare in subsoil. Surface soil, on the other hand, may contain springtails and millepedes, and should not be used unless previously heated.

Stable manure is known to contain many forms of life, and there is little doubt that some of the creatures responsible for injury to mushrooms are part of its natural fauna. The number of insects found in a heap of stable manure decreases with successive turnings, probably because the manure is gradually brought into a condition less suitable for them, and also because many of them are killed by the heat produced during fermentation, hence the belief, largely supported by experience, that efficient composting is one of the primary points in successful pest control.

116

The outer layers of a fermenting heap, however, always remain more or less at atmospheric temperature and the rise in temperature internally is slow enough to enable some proportion of the more active stages of insects and mites to migrate to regions where conditions are suitable. Eggs and other stages incapable of such migration are probably killed, though little is known about the temperatures that are fatal to many of the species concerned.

Mites

Mites are very common, but because of their small size they only attract attention when present in large numbers. Many species occur in organic debris, among animal and vegetable refuse and on straw and grain. Some are predatory, feeding upon other mites and insects, but others eat decaying plant or animal tissue, or fungi growing upon it. As a rule, predatory mites can be distinguished from others by reason of their much more rapid movements. They usually occur in numbers in stable manure and often upon mushroom beds, but their presence is simply an indication of the existence of other forms of life which are suitable food for them. The majority of predatory mites that the grower is likely to observe belong to the family *Gamasidae* (*Parasitidae*). They are pale in colour when young, but become a darker yellowish brown as they develop.

Only those species that feed upon fungi need be described. Many other species, such as those that infest grain and stored food products, occasionally occur accidentally upon mushroom beds, having been introduced in some way, but they do not attack mushrooms.

Most of the fungus-feeding mites belong to the family *Tyroglyphidae*. They are minute, soft bodied, pale, translucent creatures, sluggish in habit and inconspicuous except when congregated in numbers. They are not, as a rule, plentiful in stable manure, but there is evidence that they become much more numerous in manure that is left undisturbed and partially dries out. Very little is known, however, of their habits and distribution, and the sudden appearance of large numbers on mushroom beds just beginning to crop has not been satisfactorily explained. At least two and probably three or more species are generally concerned, but they all cause much the same type of injury, holes of various sizes being made in the caps and stalks. The two species most commonly called the Mushroom mite are *Tyrophagus longior* Gerv. (synonym *T. dimidiatus* Herm.) and *T. putrescentiae* Schr., but they are so similar in appearance that the lack of accurate descriptions makes it difficult to identify the species with certainty.

One of the most common species, *T. putrescentiae*, is well known on grain, stored foodstuffs, and cheese and it often abounds in hay and straw, from which latter source it probably gains access to mushroom beds. It is, however, widely distributed and is common on old leaves and among debris in glasshouses, and has been recorded as attacking various glasshouse plants.

Other very closely related species, *Caloglyphus* (*Cosmoglyphus*) *krameri* Berlese and *Eberhardia* sp. have also been recorded as destructive. One other species in this family, *Histiostoma feroniarum* Dufour (H. *rostro-*

serratum Megrin) often occurs in mushroom beds and upon overripe mushrooms, especially under damp conditions. It is not regarded as directly injurious in this country, but a similar mite, which occurs in America, is looked upon as a serious pest.

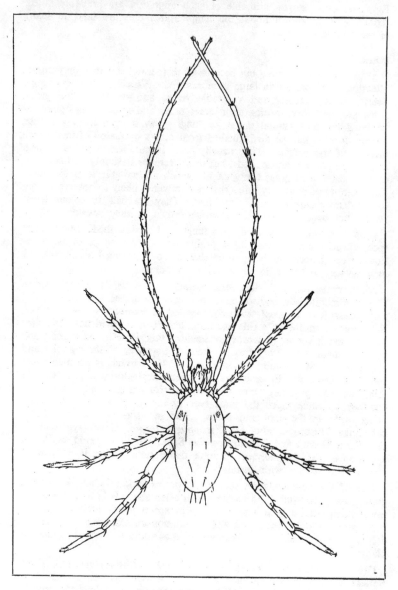

Fig. 1. THE LONG-LEGGED MUSHROOM MITE (*Linopodes antennaepes* Banks) [× 56]

CLEANING, SANITATION, AND DISPOSAL OF SPENT COMPOST

WHEN the crop is over, the houses should be cleaned out promptly to prevent accumulation of diseases and insects, and to save the bed boards. The boards should be scraped off and brushed, but washing is not necessary unless the compost had been very wet and sticky. The floor, however, must be more carefully cleaned, and washing is a good measure. In cleaning it is important to remember the advice on page 53 that all houses must be cleaned before any of the plant is filled again. The compost should be removed from the plant without delay, and must not be spread on or near any ground which is a source of casing soil.

The spent compost has the same value as fertilizer as fresh manure (of course there will be about half as many tons obtained from the house as were put into it). It is not a good humus-builder in the soil as the mushroom spawn feeds on the humus-producing compounds. Therefore it is quickly decomposed and its elements are very quickly available. In spite of its quick availability it can not burn crops, the nitrogen being in protein form. It is used on lawns, golf courses, gardens, asparagus, potatoes, and general crops. Its acid nature makes it especially good for grass and potatoes. Long-continued use produces an acid soil and lime must be used as a corrective.

The spraying of the bed boards, walls, and floor with any good fungicide is recommended if the house has been infected with serious weed molds. The treatment may be made at any time before filling. Bordeaux mixture consisting of 12 pounds of copper sulphate and 4 to 8 pounds of lime per 50 gallons water is adequate. White-wash is not to be recommended as it is not a fungicide and may easily protect mold spores against fumigation, then peel off and expose them.

At the same time the main fumigation is made, all ground in use as part of the mushroom plant and which might possibly hold spores of molds or diseases should be sprinkled with a solution of four pounds of mercury bichloride in 50 gallons of water, so that the surface is thoroughly wet. A hose may be used to keep the ground wet for a few hours afterward, so that the poison is sure to cover all the ground. This material is a deadly poison. The grower must remember that most of the chemicals he uses are poisons to people, animals, or plants, and be careful in their use. It is best for this reason to locate mushroom plants apart from gardens, orchards, or other business operations.

Two weeks before filling is the best time to make the main fumigation, as described on page 53. The houses should be clean, warm, and humid; the humidity may be raised by dampening the walls and floor, but no water should be noticeable anywhere, as it would protect spores underneath it. The houses should be sealed by pasting paper over all cracks or openings. The gas should be left in the houses two or more days.

The above treatments will prepare the houses for the new filling. They may be made while the manure is being composted, if necessary. Some extra treatments may be devised for special purposes such as Truffle control, but none are yet decided upon.

SANITATION AND PEST CONTROL

———

It is quite apparent that the home mushroom grower will be unable to use the methods of the commercial grower to control attacks from either disease or pest. Fumigating with nicotine shreds or sulphur powder would not only kill the pests but everybody in the home as well for these fumigants create highly poisonous gasses. Growing on a very small scale, such as in boxes or on tiers in the attic or cellar, will call for cleanliness and careful cultivation, but attacks from pests and diseases should not make their presence felt on anything like the same scale as with the commercial grower who has possibly 5,000 square feet concentrated under one roof. The large grower overcomes much of the trouble by " peak heat " process or pasturisation of the compost when made up into beds but here again the home grower has not the heating facilities to give this treatment. There are, however, a number of points in the aid to cleanliness that the home grower can easily do. First is sanitation of the boxes or building. A cellar or barn should be whitewashed after each crop. This will not kill disease or prevent attacks from pest but it will give the building a " sweet " smell and attractive appearance which snow-white mushrooms do deserve. If a disused stable is being used then it is advisable to cover the floor with powdered lime ; or a new preparation called Gammexane, applied as a powder or a spray will definitely kill most pests which are troublesome to mushroom beds. This is without doubt the mushroom grower's best friend for it is quite harmless to human beings (though not advisable to use it on bread and butter !), cheap and highly efficient. A small quantity, say 1 lb. to 1 ton, may be mixed in the compost at the beginning and when the beds have been made up. Another dusting of the surface will kill off any pests driven to the top. Gammexane may also be used in aerosal form but unless growing on a semi-professional scale, this will not be necessary.

Before we consider the most likely pests and diseases to

cause trouble to the small scale grower, site contamination should be discussed first. As with most crops that are cultivated indoors, soil or site sickness will gradually reduce succeeding crops to an uneconomical level, indeed outdoor conditions will be the same though a longer period will be needed to reach that level. Something then must be done to prevent such conditions from arising. It seems to be agreed that it is caused by certain organisms in the walls, bed boards or in a soil floor that in some way make their presence felt in succeeding crops of mushrooms. Large and small growers will experience the trouble as boxes which may have been used for, say, three crops without any precautions being taken may then give smaller crops. Of course, a fresh box used after two crops will prevent this trouble but will be an expensive way of mushroom growing. Where beds are made up in the open ground it will, where possible, be best to make a new bed on a new site ; where this is not possible then make sure to remove a 3″ layer of soil when each new bed is made up on the original site. Where mushrooms have not been grown on a site or in a building for at least 12 months then it may be considered safe to introduce a fresh crop without taking any precautions in contamination.

When first commencing commercial culture in 1935 I found that site-contamination was the biggest cause of crop failures. On occasions when the compost appeared in almost perfect condition, and indeed a heavy first " flush " resulted, the crop died out prematurely with no apparent reason. When I was introduced to a 5 per cent. solution of formaldehyde with which to spray walls, bed boards and floors after each crop, no further trouble resulted. Formaldehyde gas is poisonous though nothing like so fierce as nicotine or sulphur fumes. Where a person is making up a number of boxes for friends then it will be as well to wash these down two weeks before re-filling with formaldehyde or Sterizal may also be used for boxes or indoor sanitation with equally effective results though I have always relied on my old friend formaldehyde. New boxes should be treated with Cuprinol ; again two weeks should be allowed before the boxes are filled and spawned. It is, of course, an excellent plan to leave all boxes awaiting a second filling in the open air for two weeks to " weather." This will be as beneficial as all the disinfectants in the world, but if combined with one of the sterilisers mentioned, then there should be no trouble at all with contamination. I mention all this, not because mushroom growing is full of troubles from beginning to end but merely to ensure that one can keep on growing a heavy crop year after year, for that is when mushroom growing is both interesting and profitable.

Whilst the strictest attention to sanitation must always be observed, most of the worries connected with growing mushrooms may be cast aside by the correct making of the compost, care as to watering the beds, and ample ventilation at the same time excluding draughts. A wet, greasy compost will almost certainly encourage every disease the mushroom has to guard against — plaster mould, verdigris, brown spot, to name a few troubles generally resulting from badly made composts. A stuffy, over-humid atmosphere will also cause trouble in so much as it will multiply or exaggerate troubles which in a " sweet," open atmosphere will give little worry at all. Elementary rules for cleanliness, preparing the compost and care of the beds will go more than halfway to ensure a clean crop. Where one wishes to use no sterilising preparation, the use of a blowlamp moved slowly over boxes or the woodwork of tier beds will do much to kill any pests or undesirable fungus disease.

Of the most troublesome diseases and the most frequently observed are :-

    (a) Fusarium or ' damping off.'

    (b) Mycogone Perniciosa or " bubbles."

    (c) Papulaspora byssina or Brown Plaster Mould, and

    (d) Scopulariopsio fimicola or White Plaster Mould.

There are others but will rarely make themselves a nuisance.

    (a) Fusarium is a form of wilting or causes damping off in much the same way as lettuce and stock seedlings are affected. The white pin-head mushrooms turn brown and fail to mature. Over watering can cause the trouble which is why I have repeatedly stressed the need for care in watering ; in fact successful mushroom growing means careful watering from start to finish. A hard, crusty casing soil may also cause the trouble, hence a soil containing peat and a few small stones. A too-humid ventilation will encourage the trouble.

    (b) Mycogone or bubbles is a casing soil disease, and from my own experience easily the most feared of all mushroom troubles for the mushrooms take on a grotesque appearance as they mature and may emit an unpleasant smell. This is essentially a casing soil disease. Certain soils may cause the trouble, others may not, hence where soil cannot be sterilised, experiment with small areas of soil and stick to the best. Soil stored too long will often contain mycogone spores.

(c) and (d) The two Plaster Moulds are similar in appearance though entirely different in other respects. Brown Plaster Mould may appear when the compost is wet and greasy and is introduced from the compost. A well prepared compost will never produce the disease. White Plaster Mould is thought to be brought by insect pests and is not generally the result of a badly prepared compost though a strong run of spawn in a healthy compost will smother it. It may survive in a compost which has not been brought to a composting temperature of 130°F. or which has not been pasteurised, the latter process of sterilisation being quite out of range of the home grower.

It may be controlled by soaking the area as soon as observed with a diluted solution of acetic acid. The affected soil should then be removed and replaced with fresh soil after the compost has received a dusting with lime.

As this book is being written during the latter weeks of 1952, a new fungicide has appeared on the market. It is called Zibimate and gives rise to a feeling of great encouragement to mushroom growers. This fungicide was, I believe, introduced by the Du Pont Company of America and is a compound of zinc. It is applied as a dust containing 15 per cent. of the ingredient and should be dusted into casing soil at the rate of 4 ozs. to 1,000 sq. ft. of bed space. Zibimate is a selective fungicide, which means that it is able to kill off a number of diseases which are troublesome to the mushroom grower without harming the mushroom itself.

Of *Pests* which might prove troublesome, and they certainly will in hot weather if simple precautions are not taken, there are three types which we shall meet continually :-

(a) Springtails.

(b) Phorid and Sciara flies.

Of the host of other pests, only slugs to outdoor beds will cause damage and we will have something to say about these creatures later.

(a) Springtails are silvery-grey in colour and having no wings do not fly but loaf around as do lice, to which they are very similar in formation. They may be eradicated by dusting the beds with

Gammexane at intervals of a fortnight. D.D.T. powders in various forms will also eradicate them but D.D.T. must only be used in the amounts prescribed, for it is a mild poison and until more is known of its toxic effects should be used with care for it may prove to be a more potent poison than realised.

(b) The Phorid and Sciara flies may be controlled by dusting the beds with a pyrethrum powder preparation and of these I favour " Black Arrow " powder. Control is most violent and in hot July weather I have seen buckets of these flies swept up from the floor of a large mushroom house. But remember that these same dead flies may have laid their eggs in the beds which will rapidly become larvae and it is these which do the damage by feeding on the spawn threads and eating into the stem and cap of the mushrooms, often making them a mass of holes and useless for eating. For about a fortnight the larvae carry on their work of destruction before completing the cycle and becoming adult flies ready to lay *their* eggs. Every week the beds should be dusted with pyrethrum powder which is quite harmless and being white will not discolour the mushrooms.

Care must be taken at all times to ensure that if mild poisons are being used to control pests, they should only be used at the end of a flush. Personally, I never use a poison of any description. I know nicotine and sulphur and hydrocyanic acid gas (cyanide) are used by commercial growers and nurserymen, but whilst Gammexane is safe and equally effective and pyrethrum powder unbeatable for the control of flies, I want to have nothing to do with poisons. And this also goes for slug poisons. Use a non-poisonous preparation for mushrooms are food and capable of absorbing much that may be unpleasant as well as much of value. Slugs will prove troublesome in damp summer weather if precautions are not taken for they love the succulent mushrooms as much as they do the succulent June stems of dahlias.

Beds under cloches and frames may be controlled by dusting with the various control preparations, only partial control of ridge beds may be given by first removing the covers and no control can be given to field grown mushrooms.

During summer when the weather may be warm and the atmosphere humid, boxes should be removed to as cool a place as possible and should be lightly dusted with a pyrethrum preparation every week. During a very hot period I have dusted a commercial house every day to prevent pest infestations getting a hold. The cost of these powders and sprays are so small in comparison with the £/s./d. of the crop saved from larvae damage that they should be routine measures in all places where mushrooms are being grown.

Let me say that pests in minute numbers are nearly always present in mushroom beds but if stuffy, humid conditions are guarded against throughout the period of the crop, little harm will result. However, it may be that a hot July will make control most difficult, unless by using a tried preparation and it is for these occasions that this chapter is written.

CPSIA information can be obtained
at www.ICGtesting.com
Printed in the USA
BVHW071415300721
612903BV00005B/801

9 781446 523537